C000184729

The Complete Cantona

The Complete Cantona

Eric Cantona

with an appreciation by Tom Tyrrell

HEADLINE

Copyright © 1996, 1997 Headline Book Publishing

Eric Cantona's autobiography, *Cantona My Story*, copyright
© 1993 Editions Robert Laffont, S.A., Paris

Originally published in France under the title *Un Rêve
Modeste et Fou*, with the collaboration of Pierre-Louis Basse,
sports journalist for Europe 1

Translated into English and adapted by George Scanlan

The right of Eric Cantona to be identified as the Author of
the Work has been asserted by him in accordance with the
Copyright, Designs and Patents Act 1988.

First published as *The Illustrated Cantona* in 1996
by HEADLINE BOOK PUBLISHING

This edition first published in paperback in 1997
by HEADLINE BOOK PUBLISHING

10 9 8 7 6 5 4 3 2 1

All rights reserved. No part of this publication may be
reproduced, stored in a retrieval system, or transmitted,
in any form or by any means without the prior written
permission of the publisher, nor be otherwise circulated
in any form of binding or cover other than that in which it
is published and without a similar condition being imposed
on the subsequent purchaser.

ISBN 0 7472 7740 0

Designed by John Hawkins
Typeset by Letterpart Ltd, Reigate, Surrey

Printed and bound in Great Britain by
Mackays of Chatham PLC, Chatham, Kent

HEADLINE BOOK PUBLISHING
A division of Hodder Headline PLC
338 Euston Road
London NW1 3BH

Contents

Preface

I have always had idols, people I have admired and whom I still admire. In music, football, writing and elsewhere. People who have meant something to me. Also small phrases, little words, taken here and there at the whim of my mood.

People less well known also. I have always liked to listen, to look and to observe. The liberty which Jim Morrison, the lead singer of the 1960s rock group The Doors, used to symbolise always confirmed me in the feeling that I have always had of being free, tied to nothing except the great dream which is life.

Arthur Rimbaud, with his poetic images, has also had an equally great influence on me. As have the love and respect for others, and also the taste of rebellion which Léo Ferré, the anarchist, used to sing about. I think also of Marlon Brando, of Mickey Rourke, of all those fragile people who managed to remain upright, strong and great. They are the people who help you to find yourself and to refind yourself; they don't make you feel alone in this immense society which has gone money mad.

Along the road which I have been prompted to take for my pleasure I have learned a lot from them, as well as from my friends, from my family, from the street. I have learned that this strength of mind, this courage, you can find only in yourself, deeply within yourself. Certainly you should listen and give advice to others and take the advice of others but always, always be yourself.

Talking to actor Mickey Rourke, one of the men he most admires. (D. Fevre/ Presse-Sports)

Chapter One

······································

The Trawler Runs Aground

'It's a love story. It's a love story.' Eric Cantona used those words to describe his feeling for Manchester United. He had signed a new three-year contract, vowing to bring success to the club once again after helping them win the Premiership in 1993 and 1994. But there was more to the occasion than that. Eric Cantona was putting behind him the memories of a traumatic three months, a period of his career when he could so easily have walked out of football forever.

If there was a turning point in the 1994-95 season then it came on Wednesday 25 January when referee Alan Wilkie raised his arm, holding high the red card and Cantona turned to walk from the pitch at Selhurst Park, the South London home of Crystal Palace.

He was sent off for retaliation. He had not reacted solely to the challenge from Crystal Palace defender Richard Shaw moments earlier, but to a series of tackles which went unpunished, perhaps unseen, by the officials. Palace had tried to wind up Cantona and they had succeeded. So it was that early in the second half of the clash between Palace and the defending champions, Eric's spring snapped.

First a tackle caught Cantona on the ankle, then a second by Shaw seemed to be directed at his Achilles' tendon as he twisted, back to goal, to try to lay off a pass to the running Andy Cole. There were other less blatant efforts to push Eric over the brink and the longer the game went on, it seemed that he was seething inside, ready for revenge when the opportunity came.

From my commentary position high above the main grandstand I saw Cantona flinch in pain once, twice, three times and predicted to my listeners back in Manchester, following the game on Piccadilly Radio, that the Frenchman would eventually explode. I had seen it before.

Eric had always given the impression that it was perfectly in order for him to mete out his own form of retribution if he was fouled and the offender escaped punishment.

He would never cast the first stone, but woe betide anyone who did and went unnoticed. Justice had to be done and if a referee overlooked an incident Eric would turn vigilante. This did not mean a sly dig in an opponent's ribs behind the official's back, he would quite openly lunge at the offender and face the consequences.

Throughout his career Eric has stood up for what he felt were his rights. His clashes with authority are well documented but following his move from Leeds to Manchester United in November 1992, his problems slowly increased to reach a peak that night at Selhurst Park.

In his first part-season at Old Trafford he was booked only twice, one of these on his return to Elland Road. It was predictable, the crowd was hostile towards him from the moment the team coach drew up outside the ground. Hundreds of supporters waited for him to disembark chanting 'Scum, scum, scum'. By the time Cantona and his colleagues reached the sanctuary of the dressing room many were covered in spittle after their disgusting welcome.

Love turned to hate for the Leeds fans who had worshipped Cantona when he helped them to their championship in 1992. The same rule seemed to apply to the tabloid press who, on the day of his move across the Pennines, hailed Eric the hero and the signing the deal of the season. A few editions later, Ferguson was being warned that he was handling high explosives with predictions that the *enfant terrible* would be impossible to control and that he would quit Old Trafford if he did not get his own way. They said Ferguson was risking his career by taking such a gamble.

There were problems, not in that first part-season when United won the championship after a 26-year wait, but in the following campaign. They began in Istanbul in a European Cup tie described later in Eric's own words.

Cantona is escorted from the field at the end of United's stormy European Cup tie against Galatasaray in November 1993. (Empics)

It was just what his critics wanted. He was shown the red card by the Swiss referee for apparently making a gesture which was misinterpreted; he was then involved in an incident with the Turkish police. The 'sending off' came after the final whistle with the Swiss referee Kurt Rothlisberger claiming Eric made a 'V' sign towards him. 'I know exactly what that gesture means and that is why I sent him off,' he said later.

As it turned out, UEFA did not add the dismissal to Eric's record because it happened after the game, and it was not his clash with the official which landed him in hot water, but an off-the-cuff remark made a few minutes after descending into the dressing-room area at the Ali Sami Yen stadium. Speaking to a French journalist, Eric is alleged to have said something like: 'When you see a display of refereeing like that you can understand all this talk about bribery in the game.'

The remark was made to a friend, but a television sound crew picked up his words and they were broadcast throughout Europe. That was that. The incident came to light the day after the game amid claims that Cantona could be banned for anything up to five years. Eventually he was suspended for four European games for making remarks *about* the referee rather than to him.

But it was open season for Cantona hunters. It mattered not if they were armed with red or yellow cards, microphones or typewriters, their quarry was the same.

Television targeted him in January 1994, highlighting an incident at Norwich where after taking a couple of heavy knocks, he had a sly kick at an opponent, back-heeling him as the pair slid from the field. This was blown out of all proportion as the pundits held their after-match inquest. 'Is there one law for Cantona and another for the rest?'

Eric's booking that day was only his second of the season – hardly a bad record – but United's exceptional progress that season made them easy targets. They were constantly on television, which showed them warts and all. They led the Premiership, were through to the fifth round of the FA Cup and the semi-final of the Coca-Cola Cup. It was not their skill which was being questioned but their discipline.

They reached Wembley in the Coca-Cola Cup by defeating Sheffield Wednesday in two terrific displays of attacking football, but, after getting through to the FA Cup semi-final ten days later, hit stormy waters. In the Premiership they went into two away fixtures separated by just three days: struggling Swindon first, then Arsenal.

Brian Hill was in charge at Swindon, a referee who does not top the Manchester United Christmas card list. The club at one time had asked that Mr Hill should not be put in charge of any of their games following controversy over his handling of an FA Cup tie in 1989 when he failed to give a decisive goal. On this occasion, television was on United's side, but Brian Hill was not a popular choice for the Swindon match.

Again there was controversy as Hill sent off Eric Cantona for standing on John Moncur. He was correct, Eric proved that he is no angel, using Moncur as a doormat in retaliation for a fierce challenge.

He was the second United player to be dismissed in a week, goalkeeper Peter Schmeichel having got his marching orders as they beat Charlton in the FA Cup, and Alex Ferguson's control over his stars was ridiculously questioned. The Schmeichel incident was a one-off, the goalkeeper had misjudged a situation, raced from his area and not only handled the ball but brought down an opponent giving the referee little choice.

By the end of the Arsenal game United's record was three dismissals in four games. The game ended in a 2-2 draw, the same score as at Swindon, but it was not the result which made the headlines.

Eric was booked for a foul on Ian Selley, then later in the game was involved in a tangle with Tony Adams and Nigel Winterburn. This incident was greeted with howls of 'off! off! off!' from the Arsenal fans and referee Vic Callow showed a second yellow card.

Steve Bruce was one of many who backed the Frenchman: 'I thought Eric was trying to get out of the way of the tackle, never mind making one himself. I think he has been singled out and harshly treated. I know referees have difficult decisions to make – that is why I try never to get involved.'

The television pictures supported the United captain.

'There have been a lot of instances recently where video recordings have been used to show people using the elbow and such like, but why can we not use that in this case?'

Referee Callow was asked to reconsider his decision in view of the television evidence but would not change his report. Cantona was banned for five games.

United's reputation for being unruly and violent was not helped when Andrei Kanchelskis was dismissed in the closing minutes of the Coca-Cola final five days after the Arsenal game. His was a handling offence as he turned goalkeeper to give away a penalty, but four sendings-off in fifteen days was a difficult statistic to play down. Despite those problems, and the handicap of suspensions, they did the Double.

Trouble followed them into the next season. Their success made them an easy target. Alex Ferguson agreed with comments that they were the most popular club in the country and the most hated. 'We are the side everybody loves to beat.' That was evident in the summer of 1994 when they took part in the Ibrox international tournament involving hosts Glasgow Rangers, Newcastle and Sampdoria.

   Their problems began in the opening game when United faced Newcastle. The Scottish fans joined forces with the Tynesiders and, with few Manchester fans there, anti-United feeling was intense.

   Eric was the main target and Brian McClair, a former Celtic player, fared little better. They lost to Newcastle on penalties, but when they played Rangers the following day the hostility against them reached a ridiculous level.

   Eric's every touch was greeted with cat-calls and the home club's defender Stephen Pressley took the role of hero, earning wild applause whenever he dispossessed the Frenchman. Pressley was urged on by the support, and Eric took exception to a couple of challenges which the referee had ignored.

   His moment came. The ball was at Pressley's feet and Eric jumped. His wild leap was in the general direction of the Rangers man but he did not make contact. The crowd was enraged, screaming for blood…Cantona's. Up went the red card, off went Cantona, and Fergie was furious. He was not angry that his player had reacted in such a manner, but at the way the incident had been interpreted. The dismissal in a meaningless match led to him being banned for three Premiership games.

The troubles continue. Cantona is sent off at Ibrox and the Rangers fans vent their feelings. (Colorsport)

Ferguson was disgusted by the way his players had been treated and felt the crowd had influenced the referee: 'The people behind Rangers have done their best to turn this club into one of the best in the country, it is such a pity that the supporters have not moved with the times as well,' he said. That from a former Rangers player who loves the club.

So we go back to Selhurst Park where, like Swindon and Glasgow, Cantona had in his own way balanced the books. In Eric's eyes, Richard Shaw had escaped punishment so he felt he was entitled to retaliate and paid the penalty.

As he left the pitch he ran the gauntlet of the baying home supporters goading him from the grandstand. One of them, Matthew Simmons, went a step further. He made his way down the gangway from his seat somewhere below the Press Box, hurling abuse and waving a clenched fist in Cantona's direction.

Eric was walking a few paces away from United kit-man Norman Davies, who had been sent to accompany him to the dressing room and unlock the door. Suddenly he stopped, turned and made eye-to-eye contact with Simmons. He seemed to ask: 'What did you say?'

The rest is history.

'Eric Cantona has just attacked a fan! Cantona has attacked a fan! He's punched a fan in the face, first he kicked him in the chest then he smashed him in the face. This is a sensation. The police are being called in and Cantona is in big trouble.'

I have listened to the recording of my commentary on the incident many times and can hear the tones of disbelief in my voice. I had never seen anything like it and, even though I found it hard to believe, I knew from the moment Eric turned towards the spectators that he was about to take the law into his own hands. He was being insulted, his family and mother were being insulted. He could stand no more.

To make contact with Simmons, he had to step over the frost-repelling tarpaulin sheet which had been rolled up alongside the pitch, then reach over the barrier rail. It was this, rather than any skill in martial arts, which made his so-called 'kung-fu' leap necessary. Simmons was like the child slinging insults from the safety of his doorstep, but with an athletic jump Cantona made contact.

He rammed his foot into the supporter's chest forcing him backwards. Simmons got to his feet flinging punches, but a right cross from Cantona floored him again before both men were wrestled apart. Other players piled in, Peter Schmeichel pulled Eric away and led him from the scene to be soaked in hot tea flung from the grandstand. The ground was in uproar, but as far as Eric was concerned the job was done.

Selhurst Park, Wednesday 25 January 1995: referee Alan Wilkie is about to show Cantona the red card for retaliating against Crystal Palace defender Richard Shaw. (Colorsport)

The infamous 'kung-fu' kick. (Colorsport)

Cantona leaves his home the morning after the incident at Selhurst Park to be faced by a battery of cameras. (Popperfoto/Reuter)

The 1-1 scoreline meant little. The following morning the tabloids demanded Eric's head.

'Kick him out!' was the cry. Sports experts and leader writers reacted, and the world cringed at what they saw again and again on their television screens. There were demands for him to be expelled from English football, banned for years, even deported. In football parlance, the media in general went over the top, and the game reacted too.

The Football Association called a press conference and chief executive Graham Kelly announced: 'Eric Cantona of Manchester United and France has been charged with misconduct that has brought the game into disrepute. He will be given 14 days to respond before an FA Commission considers the case. What happened last night was a stain on our game. If any offence is proved, the player concerned is bound to face a severe punishment.

'We are confident that Manchester United will meet their responsibility, not just to their own club, but to the widest interests of the game. The Football Association believes last night's incident was unprecedented. It brought shame on those involved, and worst of all, on the game itself. We especially deplore the appalling example set to young supporters who are the game's future.'

Kelly told the gathering that the FA did not have the power to ban Eric immediately, but the following day, reacting to advice given to them by the

Football Association, United suspended their star until the end of the season and fined him a maximum two weeks' wages.

It was a blow to United's chances of taking the championship for a third successive season. They had begun the season steadily, but in Europe failed once again, handicapped by the UEFA 'foreign player' rule which hit British clubs more than any others.

British citizenship meant nothing; Welsh, Irish and Scottish players were regarded as foreigners. Schmeichel or Giggs, Cantona or Keane? That was Ferguson's problem and it was no surprise when United failed to qualify for the stage beyond the Champions League.

Eric's ban following the Galatasaray incident meant he missed victory over Gothenburg at Old Trafford and the chance of playing at the Ali Sami Yen once again, fate having thrown Galatasaray into the same group as United.

He returned to play against Gothenburg in Sweden in a game they needed to win to qualify for the next stage, but lost 3-1. That night, Paul Ince was sent off for arguing with the referee and, a week later at Highbury, Mark Hughes was dismissed after two bookable offences.

As Christmas approached, there was speculation that Ferguson was about to strengthen his team. Stan Collymore, the Nottingham Forest striker, kept United in second place as he helped his side to a 2-1 win at Old Trafford and afterwards made no secret of his ambitions to join a big club. But it was Andy Cole of Newcastle who was bought as Blackburn still led the Premiership early in January 1995.

Cole and Cantona was Ferguson's dream strike force and it seemed that fate was playing its part when Hughes badly gashed his knee as he scored at Newcastle in the game which followed the £7 million player-plus-cash deal. Hughes would be out for weeks and the manager had made a timely purchase, but after 140 minutes together, Cantona and Cole were separated by the nightmare at Crystal Palace.

Cole's debut was against Blackburn three days before the trip to Selhurst Park, but it was Eric who got the only goal of the game, contorting his body to head home brilliantly a Giggs cross ten minutes from time. It was the last goal Eric Cantona would score for almost nine months.

Sunday's hero became Wednesday's villain. Seventy-six hours after he had dented Blackburn's hopes of taking the title, he dashed United's by attacking Matthew Simmons.

Chairman Martin Edwards was at Selhurst Park but admitted afterwards that he had not seen the incident fully. 'It was not until next morning when I turned the television on that I saw it for the first time. I realised that something had to be done and the first thing the club had to decide was "do we keep Eric or not?"

Andy Cole and Eric Cantona, a formidable strike partnership cut short by the events at Crystal Palace. Cole made his debut against Blackburn on 22 January, but the Frenchman scored the only goal of the game. (Colorsport)

'The board decided that anybody is worth a second chance, but in granting that second chance we had to decide the severity of the punishment. Manchester United is bigger than Eric Cantona, and the game of football is bigger than Manchester United. We felt we had to set an example and make the punishment fit the crime.

'I would hope that the severity of the punishment Manchester United have dished out to the player will be taken into consideration when the commission meet.'

Wishful thinking! The witch-hunt began.

United sent Eric and his wife Isabelle on a short holiday as they looked forward to the birth of their second child, but even this caused controversy. There were claims he had ignored police instructions to attend an interview at Croydon, but Alex Ferguson stepped to his defence saying: 'Maurice Watkins, the club solicitor, explained to the police that Eric was going on holiday and nothing was said. They never gave him any appointment, never said when they wanted to interview him. I really think there has been a lack of communication on the police side of it. Eric has gone away quite innocently for the break which I felt was important to him simply because the media attention he has been getting has been horrendous.'

The Cantona home in Boothstown on the outskirts of Salford was besieged.

The press stake-out packed the roads to and from the estate making life hell for anyone living within 100 yards. If Eric or any of his family showed their faces, lenses were pointed, cameras clicked and whirred, television reporters pushed microphones towards them and questions were shouted by running journalists.

United gave out false information about the holiday destination, reporters flew to the Virgin Islands but found no Cantona. Eventually he was tracked down to Martinique by an ITN camera crew and there were allegations he had attacked their reporter in a similar way to the Simmons incident. Authorities on the island confiscated the crew's video tapes and put an end to that particular debate.

During this time, United had played three games without Eric, winning them all. They topped the Premiership for 24 hours after defeating Manchester City 3-0 at Maine Road and on the weekend the Cantonas returned home beat Leeds 3-1 to reach the quarter-finals of the FA Cup. Even without Cantona, the team was in contention for a repeat of the Double.

Skipper Steve Bruce saw it as a way of repaying a debt they owed Eric: 'He is sadly missed by us all. He's a terrific, terrific player. We all know what he has done on the pitch for us and that is how we know Eric. He has helped us enormously and if we can do one thing for him, and that is go on and have a little bit of success without him, then I am sure that we will all be delighted.

Cantona and manager Alex Ferguson in St Albans for the FA's disciplinary hearing. (Popperfoto)

'We were all a little bit shocked by what happened, but it happened. He was provoked and we have got to forget about it. The important thing is just to get on with the game because the game of football itself is the most important.'

On Friday 24 February Eric attended the Football Association's hearing at Sopwell House Hotel, in St Albans. It is not one of United's 'lucky' hotels. They stayed there before the FA Cup final in 1976 and lost to Southampton. They were losers again as Eric's ban was extended until 30 September. The disciplinary commission added its own punishment to that imposed by the club.

Martin Edwards was furious: 'People have different views on the case and all I can say is that we felt we had punished Eric heavily. Obviously, the FA felt they had to add to that ban and we are disappointed that they felt that they needed to go further than we had already gone. What is on our minds is that if we had banned Eric for example for ten games, then the FA may just have doubled that and he would have been available for the start of next season.

'Clearly people will have to judge in future how far they go with any punishment if we feel that the FA are going to add to that. It is going to make clubs think twice when they are punishing people.'

Rumour had it that a deal had been struck with the FA that if United banned Cantona until the end of that season there would be no need for further punishment. The commission had reneged on the agreement. Punished once by his club, a second time by the FA, there was more to come for Eric.

Amid speculation that he might quit England if he was severely punished, Eric faced Croydon Magistrates on Thursday 23 March. After a 50-minute deliberation chairman of the bench, Mrs Jean Peach announced: 'You have pleaded guilty to common assault and the facts that we have heard show that this is a serious offence. We have heard from your counsel that you deeply regret your actions. We have taken this into account, together with your previous good character and your guilty plea. We do feel, however, that you are a high-profile public figure with undoubted gifts and as such you are looked up to by many young people. For this reason the only sentence that is appropriate for this offence is two weeks' imprisonment forthwith.'

An immediate appeal allowed Eric his freedom, and a week later the sentence was reduced to one of community service. The judge who considered the appeal said that Simmons, who himself would later appear in the same court, had indulged in conduct which would 'provoke the most stoic'.

Arriving at Croydon Magistrates, 23 March 1995. (Colorsport)

A press conference was called and Eric stunned the media with his statement: 'When the seagulls follow the trawler it is because they think, perhaps, sardines will be thrown into the sea.'

They laughed, but inside, it was Eric who was laughing loudest. He was laughing at those who had followed in his wake for weeks hoping to pick up scraps of information on which they could gorge themselves. The media were the seagulls, and in this instance Eric was the trawler. Off the record, Maurice Watkins said Eric could have expressed the same sentiment in two words.

A barrage of microphones had been mounted in front of him, notepads were opened in anticipation, tape recorders rolled but another sixteen months elapsed before Eric spoke of the incident.

In an interview for *Hello!* magazine he revealed: 'The hardest thing was having to put up with the endless comments, the swift judgements, the resounding criticism. My family were quite shocked but they were also there. Every time I go through this kind of experience, I react in the same way. First I feel like going away, forgetting it all, escaping. Very quickly pride, and maybe even a deep sense of honour, urges me to take action. Then I can stand tall and face up to it. Then you have the kids to keep in mind, they are my strength.'

Raphaël was only six at the time of the Crystal Palace incident, and Eric was aware of the problems his son faced at school: 'You can imagine children of that age. Kids can be really cruel. They don't give each other much of a chance.

'Every day he heard: "Your father is this, or that…" When he came home at night he would ask: "Daddy, is it true you're a this or that…?"

'I had to explain all the time, reassure him, give him arguments so that he would not be helpless the next day at school. It is very important to talk with one's children especially when there is a problem. It is no use hiding things. Isabelle was pregnant at the time, she proved she was very strong too.'

Daughter Joséphine was born as Eric served out his 120 hours of community service under the watchful eye of the Salford Probation Service. His punishment was to coach hundreds of schoolchildren; he liked it so much he continued beyond the time limit imposed by the courts.

'I was entrusted to take care of several hundred children from a rough neighbourhood. Well, I had to do it, but I wanted to go even further. Quite unexpectedly I found myself going beyond the stipulated commitment. I devoted myself to those kids, which has improved the rapport with the club. I hope I did bring some light into their lives. I did it for them, but for me as well.'

There was still speculation he would quit England, driven out by the media hawks but it was to the children he was coaching that he gave the first real clue about his plans for the future. Ten-year-olds from Ellesmere Park Junior football team in Salford were the first to attend the sessions in United's indoor training area. Afterwards they breathlessly revealed: 'He taught us a lot of football skills and we asked him if he would stay at Old Trafford, he said that he would try his best. We all said we hoped he would stay.'

So did the club. Contract talks were held with chairman Edwards as the newspapers continued their guessing game. The majority seemed to feel Eric would quit, but on Friday 28 April, United called their own press conference. With Cantona present it was obvious it had not been organised to announce his departure. He had in fact agreed a new three-year deal.

'I am staying here because Manchester United is the biggest club in England, maybe in Europe, maybe in the world and I am very pleased to have the opportunity to win again many trophies with them. Everybody at this club deserves it and all the fans too.'

During the period the contract talks were under way, United faced Crystal Palace again, this time in the semi-final of the FA Cup. Controversy reared its head when reports came through that a Palace supporter had been killed outside a Walsall public house. Immediately, newspapers jumped to conclusions with suggestions of rioting United fans seeking revenge for the Simmons incident. It later materialised the fan had tragically fallen under the wheels of a coach.

United reached the Cup final after a replay, but in the Premiership were six points adrift of Blackburn Rovers. If ever Eric's help was needed it was now. Alex Ferguson was delighted and relieved that his star player was remaining at Old Trafford, even though he knew that there might be problems when he eventually returned.

Ferguson:
We were never going to win no matter what we did. I think what we have done has pleased our own fans and pleased Manchester United, the players and everybody associated with the club. In doing that we have taken a giant step towards winning things by sealing Eric's future for the next three years. Watching the situation since January, how he has handled the whole thing, we know that he has always wanted to stay here. I think that was important for Eric as much as it was for us.

   He has never had one complaint about the punishment. He never says a word about it, he has just got on with life and it has taken tremendous courage from him to do that. There's not many people could handle that.

It was obvious that the club was angered at the extension to his suspension.

Ferguson:
I don't think there will be any player ever in the history of football who will get the sentence that he got. I think it is so severe. But he has handled that so well that you have to admire a lot of that. Also the fact that he wants to play for Manchester United is important.

Eric told those convinced he would quit:

Cantona:
I am here, I am with Manchester United and I can forget everything, and we can win everything. We are bigger than the people who have sometimes been so hard and sometimes so wrong. That is not a problem. For me it is not a problem.

He admitted that his tolerance had been stretched to the limit and that there were times when he felt he might leave.

Cantona:
Yes, I thought about it, it was a difficult moment for me when I thought that, but it was a very short moment. Now I would like to spend the rest of my career here. The support of the manager and everybody who loves Manchester United was important. It is a compliment for me when people speak about me even when it is hard. You fear me much more than I fear you.

Could he cope with the provocation he would face on his return: 'Easily, yes, easily.'

The matter was settled. Eric was staying, and ended the conference on a light note. Looking at his watch he said: 'You will have to forgive me. I must go, we have got the training and I need to be fit for my next game in October!'

He made a smart exit, and, although I did not realise it at the time, gave me the only one-to-one interview he would agree to for the next year when he explained to me how special Manchester United is to him: 'It's a love story, it's a love story. I cannot say more than that it is very strong.' His affection for the people of Manchester played its part also: 'That and the level of the club. It is one of the biggest clubs in the world and I couldn't leave.'

The season ended in disappointment. Blackburn pipped United to the title on the closing day of the campaign and, six days later, United lost to Everton in the FA Cup final. But, for Cantona, there was the future to look forward to. He could continue with his love story, which had begun many years before in Caillols.

Banned from playing until October, Cantona is forced to watch the 1995 FA Cup final from the bench. (Popperfoto)

Chapter Two

∙ ∙

The Sunshine of Caillols

Few people remain as close to their families as Eric Cantona. In a June 1996 edition of Hello! *magazine, to celebrate his 30th birthday, he was portrayed relaxing with his parents, Albert and Eleonore, his brothers Joël and Jean-Marie and their families, and his wife Isabelle and their children, Raphaël and Joséphine, at the family country retreat in the Alpes de Haute Provence. He is clearly very much at home, and his autobiography shows why the farm and their house in Caillols hold such a special place in his heart to this day.*

I am a son of rich people.

But with us riches have never been money or luxury or even expenditure. Frankly, I wish that all those children who ask for my autograph were able to have the same values which were transmitted to me by my family in the hills of Marseille. That would be a great start in life.

I was born in springtime, 24 May 1966. Within a couple of months England wins the World Cup at Wembley thanks to the goalscorer Geoff Hurst, to Bobby and to Jackie Charlton and to the one they call 'The Flying Goalkeeper', Gordon Banks. On 30 July, in front of 100,000 spectators, they defeat West Germany and Hurst scores three goals. England wins 4-2 and London celebrates. They celebrate also from Land's End to Carlisle and places far beyond.

It is 1966. Gaston Deferre has already been in charge at Marseille for more than 20 years. The one who 20 years later will become my wife, Isabelle, is somewhere in the streets of Orange. The small girl runs in the sun. The Beatles have long left their Cavern in Liverpool, where they made their debuts in the middle of blocks of redbrick flats. Their song 'Paperback Writer' will soon be a massive hit around the world. Gérard Philippe, the biggest star of the 1960s in France, captures the hearts of the young girls. The Russians send missiles, rockets and men around the earth.

It is then, three years after Jean-Marie, one and a half years before Joël, that I turn up in the *arche* of the Cantonas. While I write this book, I can find no other word capable of describing my childhood home. The Larousse dictionary defines *arche* as: 'A house where all sorts of individuals live together especially as a family – all of the family – in other words father, mother, children and grandchildren.'

Even today, the people who live in Caillols ask themselves how was it possible for the Cantonas to manage to build this home, overlooking the region and nestling high up a mountain. But they say that only because they don't know the courage and strength of my grandfather Joseph, who was a mason by trade.

It has to be said that our house is very unusual. It was Lucienne, my paternal grandmother who, during the summer of 1955, discovered the place as she went about the region buying and selling and doing small trade. It was situated on the boundaries of the 11th and 12th arrondissements of Marseille and she moved in there with Joseph and their only son, Albert. They made their home in a cave of nine square metres, which became a well known and unusual talking point in the village. By the time I was born, this cave was only one room in the house, with the rest of the building above it.

Families from the centre of Marseille go off and picnic every Sunday on the hill so as to enjoy the view. Yet I had it spread out in front of me for the whole of my childhood. It is one of the most beautiful sights that one can imagine: we looked out over the town to the distant hills of Gardaban and Cassis. In good weather it was possible for me to see the first rows of houses of Aubagne, Saint-Marcel and la Vierge de la Garde in the distance.

During the war the Germans chose this area as their headquarters, because it dominated the region, and even used our cave as a lookout point when they arrived in 1940. But my grandparents' first winter in Marseille, in 1955–6, was cold, the worst in living memory. Only a curtain separated the room from the outside. One day the exit from the cave was barred by snow and my grandparents could get out only after working all day to clear the snow.

However, the cold and the damp were not enough to put the Cantonas off their Mediterranean cuisine. Trapped inside, my grandmother improvised, cooking pastries for dinner in the melting snow. While he ate them, my grandfather recalled how he had lived in the boulevard Oddo, which was a gathering point for all the families of Italian immigrants who disembarked at Marseille. As a child at home, Joseph used to speak Sardinian, the language of his parents.

After this terrible cold spell, my grandparents began enlarging the house and today the cave has developed into a family home, but it is also still very cramped – a legacy of a house which has been enlarged and expanded over the course of years. The cave is now a small bedroom.

My father has not forgotten this time when his family could not escape from the cave. Before coming to Caillols as a child, he had discovered in the castle of Gambert the perfumes of the Provençal countryside. His love of the rural atmosphere grew from that period. So as, in those days, this part of the twelfth arrondissement of Marseille was surrounded by fields, he developed a strong passion for hunting and walking his dogs.

To live in Marseille, when one is not rolling in money, is like living in Barcelona, Algiers or Casablanca: there is always the sunshine, the hills and the sea to enjoy. Money is not vital in such circumstances.

Very young and very quickly my brothers and I learned that we would never be children left to their own devices. With us the word 'family' has always had a special meaning. We would always dine together – even at the end of the month when money was short and there was less to eat. One event, more than any other, made me promise never to betray this spirit as I began to raise my own family. I had arranged to meet my brother Joël in Carcassonne one morning in October 1991 for an early hunting session. I was very surprised to see him arriving in his suit, looking sombre and preoccupied. 'Pépé died this morning,' he said to me.

The stadiums of the world could have crumbled. I had just lost the one person who had been the guiding light of my youth, my inspiration – Joseph. Nothing had any real importance for me now. I thought of my grandmother, whose curiosity and *joie de vivre* were going to be shattered at a stroke. For several years we have met up in the small village where he lived in the Hautes Alpes, having moved out some time ago so that my parents could take over in Caillols. It is there, at the foot of the mountain, that the mason Joseph lies at rest. Rest in peace, Pépé, we will all go to the village this year as usual – to see Lucienne and to visit her husband's grave in the family vault that she had built.

As well as the sun, the main memory of my childhood, which comes back to me very, very often, is the happiness of sport. Like most of the boys of Marseille, I didn't wait to be too steady and too secure on my legs before kicking anything which resembled a football. In Marseille, a brilliant white town full of light, all the children play ball in the street.

And I was no different. I was attracted to ball games very early in my life. Both at the infants' school of Caillols and then later when I was at the Grande Bastide secondary school in Mazargue, it was my good fortune to be able to count on my two brothers to play with. Between us, we formed a very effective trio.

Just like Jean Tigana and Roger Jouve before me, I discovered football at the club of Caillols. This is the well-known junior team based in the suburbs of Marseille, only a ten-minute bus ride from the centre. The club provided

Cantona inherited his love of painting from his father. (Colorsport)

training and organised football matches for boys from the age of five to fifteen. Those early years were very valuable experience for me. The streets and the fields did the rest.

Imagine the cool, light evenings in summer in Marseille. With my friends Galtier, Falzon and many others, we gave the doors of the garages in our district, which served as our goals, such a battering that they still bear the marks.

I must admit that football in the streets gave us a great sense of freedom and liberty. There's nothing surprising in the fact that our heroes learned football in the open fields and on the streets. Look at Skoblar and Salif Keita and, later, the little boy with golden feet, Maradona, or even Platini. All of them have dribbled tin cans and aimed them at imaginary goals before they had their opportunity to make the stadiums of the entire world explode with happiness.

When I first learned to play football in Caillols, I was a goalkeeper – undoubtedly because my father had always been a keeper too. But when I decided finally to play out, my father, who loved football, never ceased to give me useful advice.

From primary school I used to go and join him in his workshop. I played at his side while he continued to do his painting. It was then that I discovered the world of colours. I took such joy from it that I often go back to it with great pleasure. When hunting and painting didn't take my father's time, his other great love was for football. One evening, when our team lost at Caillols, however, I experienced for the first time some doubt about the game, more horrible than the bitterness of defeat, when my father criticised the way I played.

He had commented: 'There is nothing more stupid than a footballer who pretends to be more indispensable to the game than the ball. Rather than run with the ball, make the ball do the work, give it and look quickly. Look around quickly and you will be the best.'

That evening I had some difficulty in understanding his point because I was very impressed by the superb dribbling of an Algerian friend with whom we played. As a little boy, he was the type of player who used to be the dominant one among us. With Jean-Marie and Joël, from the age of eight years, we always tried to see who could keep the ball longest. That, rather than passing it, was seen as being important. Now I had to learn the skill of passing properly.

'There is nothing more simple than football,' my father said. 'Look before you receive the ball and then give it and always remember that the ball goes quicker than you can carry it.' That evening I cried. But I was only just beginning my football apprenticeship.

My best days and my best moments were those which I spent with my brothers on the beach near Estaque where we used to spend our summer holidays with the family. Then, as a child, I learned about how much stupidity and injustice there was all around.

It was in the summer of 1978 and I shall never forget it. I was with my friends Galtier, Falzon, Bertoli, the 'colts of Caillols', and our team had just won the Cup of Provence. I was very proud to take part in this victory in the final at the expense of Vitrolles, whom we beat 3-0. But the celebration wasn't going to last very long.

The cup triumph had set us up for a possible league and cup double. Caillols went into the final game needing only to draw with Vivaux-Marronniers to clinch the title and secure our dream. Unfortunately, although we had dominated the game, Vivaux were leading 1-0 with five minutes left to play. In the stands, my grandmother Lucienne, who never missed a match, was upset at our performance. Protected from the sun by her ever-present umbrella, which she often used to shake, I knew that she was watching me.

It was at this moment that I chose to set off from defence and dribble towards the opponent's goal. I took on a good half-dozen players – it could not have been better in a dream. I was alone, just a few feet from goal and if I scored we would surely be champions this evening.

But the referee blew up because my bootlaces were undone. The rule is a formality: a footballer must have his laces tied.

The match is over and tears are flowing in the dressing room.

I soon forget this cruel disappointment. In the evening on my bed, below the posters of Bruce Lee, I fall asleep dreaming of the white shirts and navy blue socks worn by my idols, Skoblar and Magnusson of Marseille.

From the age of 11 I have imagined myself leading a savage and invincible horde of Dutch footballers. I am at once Neeskens, Cruyff, Repp or Arie Haan. That was more than just a mere football team. I have always believed that the Dutch finalists in the World Cup in 1974, beaten 2-1 by West Germany, was a family whose 11 brothers had always played together. Johan Cruyff apart, whose elegance and style were without compare, the other players, with their hair down to their shoulders, all looked the same.

I must admit that I slept very little the night of 7 July 1974 because the victory of Breitner, Maier, Beckenbauer, and the joy of the Olympic stadium of Munich seemed to me a dark betrayal of the beautiful play of the Dutch. Four years later, in Buenos Aires, the betrayal was repeated. This time Holland was beaten in the final by Argentina. My attachment to the Dutch play was so strong that in 1982 I was almost on the point of wanting them to win against France in the Parc des Princes.

Between the workshop where my father helped me to discover his painting and his passion for Van Gogh and the football fields, my destiny would rest forever on the shoulders of two men: my father and Célestin Oliver, the former international who became a teacher at the secondary school of Grande Bastide in Mazargue and who was the first one to convince me that my strength, if you can say that, was not only as a footballer. I was also different.

This man had taken part in the trip to Sweden for the 1958 World Cup with the French national team. His power on the field of the stadium of Caillols had a kind of legitimacy acquired by heroes who return from wonderful battles. Without doubt it was he who discovered that I had a driving need for success. With all the means at his disposal at school, Célestin Oliver pushed me towards victory, without betraying the beautiful game.

In France, the clubs recruit players as young as 14. For Cantona, his early associations with professional clubs did not go well, but soon he found a club and a manager who offered him the security and support he needed, especially as he was to move far from his home and his family. Cantona remembers those days:

I was a Marseillais, attached to the perfumes and smells of the hills of Provence, to the passions of a warm and sensual town. I was incapable of imagining that I could say farewell to the sea and the sun. But at the age of 14 it seemed to me that one day or another I would have to choose between

31

my trade and my home town. Would this be the beginning of a long voyage across the footballing map of Europe?

I was convinced that to succeed I would have to go away and abandon, at least for a short time, all that I had loved ever since I could remember. Frankly, I wasn't taking any risk in shocking my family because, even though I was young, I didn't have to be a magician to know the path which my grandparents had taken.

My father's family originated in Sardinia, while my mother's came from Spain. I had never forgotten that Pedro Raurich, her father, had defied the Falangists in the arid plains of Catalonia. Seriously wounded in 1938, the young Spanish Republican had been forced to go back to France in order to be treated. This officer, 30 years old, was fiercely opposed to the Spanish clergy and to the dictatorship which Franco imposed on Spain for 40 years, chose France rather than the United States as his land of exile. With his young companion Paquita, just 17 years old, they were to begin a long journey towards the concentration camps set up in Vichy in the heart of the Massif Central, before being deported to Saint-Priest.

At the end of the war Pedro, who had worked on building the dam of Saint-Etienne de Cantales, set up house in Marseille. France was free once more, but on the other side of the Pyrenees an old general continued to muzzle and to lock up those who opposed his regime. Like many Spaniards, my grandfather was never to see his parents again. It seemed to me that, in comparison with such an exile, I could allow myself to leave Marseille, at least for a short time.

I believed that my father also held within him a secret desire for adventure, but the constraints of family life hadn't ever allowed him to satisfy it fully. Instead of being able to see the world, he had had to escape through his painting. I, too, was ready to see more of the world.

It was 1981 and I was about to move to Nice Football Club because it was based not very far from my house. At the age of 14, it's never very simple to pack up and go. I was going to Nice, encouraged by the advice of my teacher and mentor, Célestin Oliver, and excited at the idea of belonging to the club of Jouve and Katalinski.

I came back disappointed.

When one is so young one has the right to be sad for petty reasons. Those in charge at Nice didn't give newcomers any pennants and didn't give me a jersey. I had to buy them. However, when, several weeks later, I was coming back from Auxerre, nearly 100 miles south-east of Paris, where I had been called by Serge Dubord and Guy Roux, I came back with my arms loaded with treasures. Those in charge of Auxerre had also graciously given me several football shirts. The journey from Marseille might have been nearly

400 miles, but I felt closer to home than I had at Nice.

The history of French football has since shown that Guy Roux is a very shrewd person. When I returned from my first visit to Burgundy, my decision had already been made: I would go and play at Auxerre.

At that age I, like most others, was very sensitive to the environment and the atmosphere of a place, and also to the personality of the trainer because, even if I would not say it to my friends, the prospect of leaving my family made me cringe. Few would honestly deny that they felt the same way.

In giving me the red striped shirt of Auxerre, with the inscription of the club's sponsors '*Chaillotine*' on it, the team's trainer achieved his object of convincing me to stay without having to say anything. I felt welcome.

I have never forgotten the sight of those fields of rape everywhere on either side of the train which took me towards Marseille. The rape fields and the cows grazing in the meadows of Auxerre, the sweetness of the hills of Morvan – they all signified that I was going away for good from the sunshine of the land of my upbringing.

When one is proud and happy at having made a difficult choice, one doesn't feel any physical pain. On my journey home from Auxerre I had spent all night in the train and was suffering from growing pains. On arriving at my house I looked more like a Provençal statuette broken in two than a young and ambitious footballer.

Guy Roux had given me 15 days to make up my mind. But that morning, pushing open the bedroom door of my parents, it wasn't me that he had to convince.

'Why are you going so far away, hundreds of kilometres from your family? Look where Nice is on the map, quite near to Marseille. Your mother and I would be able to come and see you each weekend.'

I was going to need good arguments because my big brother was also asking why I was getting ready to pack my bags and go. I knew exactly what it was that my parents wanted, but I also knew that I had to go. It was necessary to leave the south and all those people I had grown up with at school. 'Look at Marsiglia. He grew up in Caillols but he didn't hesitate to go to Boulogne-sur-Mer. And it's going well for him. You know quite well that the majority of players from the coast don't ever impose themselves unless they leave home. Me, I want to succeed. And to succeed, I must go.'

My father did not insist. I understood that at the first telephone call he would be able to come to Auxerre with my mother to see me and if need be to encourage me.

I just had time to celebrate my birthday with my family but the party could not be prolonged because, from the end of May 1981, I was taking part in my first training sessions with Auxerre.

That summer of 1981, the atmosphere in the dressing rooms at the ground of the Abbé Deschamps and the warmth of the hostel where we stayed during the week gave me great happiness. I had the impression that this club was paying attention to me and looking after me.

There's nothing more fabulous than changing town and environment while keeping one's bearings in search of the ultimate goal. What did it matter that the sky was grey or, even worse, that I was living so far from Caillols? Auxerre had been in the first division for over a season, Guy Roux was offering me both a change and security. At one stroke, I did not want to have any more contact with the people of the south. I felt that if I was going to succeed I had to leave quickly and not lose any time.

What can you say about the strength and obstinacy of a young man when he has come to a decision…

I was just 15 and I was getting ready to leave the bosom of the family. I was leaving so many things behind me, not least going hunting with my father and brothers in the early hours of the morning. I had another look at everything – it is only at the moment when the door opens that one can know how much one is attached to a place, a house or to a family.

My father had always enjoyed hunting. Nature intoxicated him. We rose at dawn to hunt the lark, woodcock and thrush. But our pleasure came from something else, what my father called 'the beauty of the hunt': the colours of dawn, pointer dogs, the smell of the wood, of the soil and the soothing sounds of nature.

But now I was leaving the hunt. I was also abandoning the matches with my friends Galtier, Bertoli and Falzon, and our swimming sessions on Wednesdays near the family house. Yes, I was leaving all this, but I was convinced that one day or another I would return and I would bring the crowd to their feet in the north and south stands of the Marseille stadium where I used to go as a little boy, sitting on the shoulders of my father.

My life was moving from one high point to another. It was only several weeks before that I was chosen as one of the best 15 schoolboys in France and now I was permitted to be alongside and sometimes to play with some of the best footballers in the league during training matches.

Looking back now, many years later, I remember that my joy during the whole of my career at Auxerre had no connection with the money that I was able to earn. How proud I was to take part in matches counting for the championship of France's first division. What joy to know that the managers of such an up-and-coming club didn't hesitate to place their confidence in a young player they had previously loaned to Martigues in the second division.

In 1981, Auxerre had just finished its first season in the first division. Guy

Roux hadn't regretted signing the striker Szarmach from Poland. He was an exceptional player, cool and modest, who single-handedly had ensured his club stayed in the first division at the end of the season. With my friends Marc Savrot, Patrick Monier, Eric Durand, we knew what a long road sown with difficulties we would have to cover to do as well. More than a dozen years have passed since my arrival in Burgundy. None of the 'Three Musketeers', as we called ourselves, is playing in the first division, though Durand has recently signed professional forms for one side. I was lucky – many promising youths fail to make the grade. Sadly, this was true of Monier and Savrot.

Guy Roux is a man who likes challenges. He knows that one or two confrontations annually between the young players of the club and the team in the first division can show up one or two of the established stars. That is why, without doubt, I began to exist in the eyes of Guy Roux one fine day in the spring of 1982. There is, in anyone's career, call it what you will – a trigger point, a stage, a revelation – it doesn't matter, but it's a magic day.

The club was finishing its second season in the first division, three years after playing in the final of the French Cup against Nantes. Guy Roux organised a match, involving players from the lower teams against the likes of Bats, Szarmach, Garande – the club's stars. When I went on in the second half it wasn't my intention to show anybody up. I only wanted to play and to play well – nothing more. The defender Lucien Denis, 15 years older than I am, will remember the miseries which I caused him that day. Off-balance, the defender tried to foul me at every opportunity. His team-mates let him know about it quite gently because you don't try to rough up somebody who's making his debut and is just trying to show his ability. But, I thought, one half of magic under the eyes of Guy Roux would help me all the same.

I was still only 15 and I had just won my place in the fourth team. Life was beautiful. However, a certain

At Auxerre Cantona was admired - and envied - for his precocious talent. (Empics)

astonishment began to show itself among the majority of players who were older than I was. I was only a second-year apprentice and was the youngest in the group, yet the following year I got into the third team where there were a number of players aged between 18 and 19 and they didn't understand how anyone could have confidence in a youngster of 16.

I didn't let it worry me. I was selected at the end of 1982 for the French youth team and I began to feel and dream that I could make it as a player. Imagine, I might even earn my living out of the game! How thrilled I was to watch the stars of the French national team, with whom we were sharing the same hotel in Lyon in June 1982.

On the eve of playing a friendly match against Switzerland as a curtain-raiser to the France-Bulgaria international match, we watched the future heroes of Seville with great respect. Platini, Giresse, Tigana had not yet played that diabolical World Cup semi-final against West Germany when the German goalkeeper got away with a horrendous foul on Battiston. But, in our adolescent eyes, their prestige was already considerable.

On the next day at Gerland, we defeated the Swiss 3-2 and I scored the third goal for the French team. We all dreamed that one day we would be able to pass over to the other side of the curtain which divided the Blues from the juniors in the hotel.

Bernard Ferrer, nicknamed 'Nino', comes to Auxerre from Vichy. It is the autumn of 1983.

He was not the only one to begin to feature in my college life: the small girl who was playing without any worries in the roads of Orange some years before is none other than his sister. Isabelle had grown up, and she was then studying at the University of Aix-en-Provence. During her holidays she came to the Chablis region to revise for her exams. I was just 17 and Isabelle was 20.

Before going into the army to act the fool, I spent a lot of time with Nino. Auxerre were third division champions of France in 1983–4 (the third division in France is made up of the reserve teams from the first division) and Guy Roux was reassured about the future of his club, the more so because I scored 20 goals and was the second highest goalscorer behind Ferrer.

At the age when youngsters go their different ways, Guy Roux decided to give me a taste of football in the first division. On 22 October 1983, Auxerre were playing against Nancy in the 18th league match of the season. I was on the field alongside the Polish player Szarmach. Garande, his striking partner, had been going through a bad patch where he struggled to score, and Guy Roux had put him on the substitute's bench to provoke a response. I did not know Szarmach well, but his simplicity, gentility and humility reassured me.

I discovered that he was not only a footballer of great talent but also a man of class. We were leading 4-1 and the Polish international had only one idea in his head: to let me score a goal. I didn't manage to do so, but my lasting memory of the game came at the end of the match with a move from defence, improvised in the circumstances, when I received a ball in my own penalty area. Without lifting my head, I slipped the ball between the legs of the attacker who had come to tackle me. Sheer insolence and instinct!

The season was coming to an end, as they say, on a high. I had partnered Szarmach, Bats and Cuperly against Nancy and then against Lens; I had played with my mate Nino in the reserve team, the champions of their league. In short, I was on cloud nine.

Guy Roux, who had never had a great liking for anything military, suggested that I responded as quickly as possible to the call to arms. In France, one year of national service is compulsory on reaching the age of 18. He told me that, as a year in the army would in any case be an absolute waste of time, I might as well waste that time by enjoying myself. We knew quite well that the square-bashing and the night treks in the cold would not be kept for us. The Joinville battalion, for top-quality sportsmen, is first of all a formidable school of fun. Based at Fontainebleau, near Paris, it was one of several sports sections in the national service. With Nino, I got ready to pass a year sleeping the day away and enjoying the night life. I was sure it wouldn't be a sad experience!

A top-class footballer sleeps, eats, plays and travels without having the time to appreciate the country through which he is journeying. By the time they are 20 years old, most players are engaged or married. For the group that gathered in the battalion, it was vital to let off steam then before renewing our acquaintance with a more sane and balanced existence.

I sometimes ask myself if these several months of vacation contributed to my success, because it is important to understand that I still had to go back to Burgundy at the end of each week to play in matches under the watchful eye of Guy Roux.

I now understand much better why the manager of Auxerre encouraged me to do my military service as quickly as possible. Excesses at the age of 18 and 19, before the true start of a career, can be easily handled by the body and are less likely to disrupt the rest of one's career.

As well as playing at Auxerre, I was also involved with the French Army side, which played widely abroad. On one such journey, to Libreville (on the equator of the west coast of Africa), I had my first experience of Africa. It was my first foreign tour with the Army team: a week in Gabon. This is the Africa which loves celebrations and shows great hospitality to newcomers. The country of Omar Bongo was no different from the rest in this matter.

It was a memorable experience and everyone went out of his way to make our stay enjoyable. I recall with pleasure the river excursions which were arranged for us on long slim boats carved locally out of tree trunks and steered by some kind of rudder at the back. We were young and the evenings were long and warm; it was natural that we would slip out of our hotel to find some nightlife. Of course this was not the best preparation for our daily training and the two matches we played against African opponents. I remember that they showed great skill with the ball and were only short of tactical awareness, but it was clear Africa would soon become a great footballing nation.

By the end of the season in 1985, Cantona was on the brink of establishing himself in the Auxerre side. But it was the wedding of his friend Bernard Ferrer that was to provide an opportunity for him to meet once more the woman who has been by his side ever since, Isabelle. He recalls this period when a new world was opening up for him:

At the end of the 1984–5 season Guy Roux was still dreaming about Europe. It is 28 May and we are in Strasbourg on the eve of a match in the Meinau stadium. A fortnight earlier in Rouen I had scored my first goal in the top division and I was full of confidence. But it was on that evening that I made my choice as to how I would live my life. I was just 19, and I was conscious of what was at stake in this match but the phrase 'healthy living' – the need for recuperation, preparation, psychology of a match – did not form part of my vocabulary. So, with Nino, I left the hotel for a brief nocturnal stroll in the streets of Strasbourg.

The next day and Guy Roux is anxious. After an hour of play, the 25,000 spectators who have come to the Meinau stadium sense victory. Strasbourg lead 1-0. For Auxerre, Europe begins to fade away into the distance, unless… Unless a young and complete unknown can restore hope.

Some minutes before the end, I get the ball in my own penalty area. Great spaces seem to open up before me and there is very little pressure on me, so I attack. I am marching towards Europe; I am sure of myself. The equaliser has not yet been scored, but I feel that something very important is going to happen. That explains our love for the game. From that moment everything changes in my life. From 25 metres I strike. The ball ends up in the top right corner of the Strasbourg goal and this goal will send Auxerre into Europe.

The night before the match, with my friend Nino, we had got back to the hotel at four o'clock in the morning. Think what you will…

We had once and for all burned all that remained of our adolescence and, for me, Strasbourg constituted the finest and final episode in a series that had begun a year earlier in the barrack room of the battalion. Starting national service had helped me to grow up.

But the film had no reason to continue any longer. As the director, I had called 'Cut!' You don't have to be very shrewd to understand that such a way of life couldn't be combined in the long term with success. The joke had lasted long enough. Nino was going to get married. It was time to put our house in order.

Guy Roux had given me a clear indication that he wanted to put me in the first team next season. I felt ready to meet all challenges. But I did not know that, as a guest at the marriage of my friend Bernard Ferrer, I would again meet his sister – and she was going to change my life. But with Isabelle it wasn't simply a case of meeting again. The young literature student from Aix-en-Provence had, like myself, something in mind. Guy Roux wasn't going to take long to notice that either. Too bad for the football, but it was the end of my Bohemian life.

Isabelle 'changed my life'. (Colorsport)

· ·

In the Big Time

A bad bout of flu can have incalculable consequences. The season of 1985 had been going for several weeks. I was ill and couldn't make the journey to Nice and was replaced up front by Roger Boli. There are substitutes who cannot fulfil their role and others who fit perfectly into the scheme of things. The brother of Basile, the current French side's defender who scored Marseille's winner in the European Cup final in 1993, belonged to the second category.

Auxerre played well that day and won at Nice. What's more, Roger Boli scored. Why change a winning side?

At the beginning of September, Auxerre welcomed AC Milan to the Abbé Deschamps stadium for the first leg of the first round of the UEFA Cup. Auxerre won 3-1 and Boli again played very well. It's not easy for a player, whatever his temperament, to sit on the sidelines as a spectator and watch the victory of his own team, especially at the beginning of a career.

Auxerre did not go far in the UEFA Cup that year. At the San Siro we were beaten 3-0 and I finally got on in the second half but could do nothing to turn it round. The sweeper for AC Milan was Franco Baresi, whose reputation as one of the best defenders in Europe was still growing. Obviously, there was sadness in the dressing room but we were not too downhearted. The team was young, with a lot ahead of it and it was our first appearance in European competition for several seasons.

Several days after this defeat by the Italians, Guy Roux came up to me and made a suggestion: 'Martigues aren't playing too well and they need you just till the end of the season. Will you go and play for them?'

I still hadn't signed my first professional contract and the prospect of going to play in the second division didn't really appeal to me.

'For how long?' I asked.

'We will only loan you to Martigues. You will give them a hand and then come back at the end of the season.'

At that moment I saw in my mind's eye the image of my girlfriend. The manager of Auxerre, by suggesting that I go and take a breath of fresh air in Martigues, had enabled me to rejoin Isabelle in Aix-en-Provence. I didn't hesitate. And thank you, Guy Roux!

Later, Isabelle told me that the scheme had been put into operation by the one who is called by his enemies 'the horse dealer'. However, his plotting in this instance was wholly to the good for all concerned. I do admit that I didn't expect the green light from Guy Roux to love a young lady whom I considered to be much more than a simple passing distraction. Isabelle was no longer a little girl and my age of 19 didn't stop me in any way knowing what I wanted to do. Some weeks after the marriage of her brother Nino, Isabelle had come to spend a fortnight with me in my apartment where I lived alone. I certainly have never forgotten the visit, nor the moment when she was about to go back to Marseille when she jumped from the train onto the platform as it began to pull away and stayed for another two days.

There are towns which are so sprawling that a manager risks wearing out his shoes trying to find out what the players are doing after training. In Auxerre, which has about 50,000 inhabitants, Guy Roux managed to find out everything. He is a man capable of going around on his moped and checking half a dozen nightclubs in the countryside so that he could sleep in peace. Guy Roux knows all his players and what he doesn't know he can imagine.

On her return to Aix-en-Provence after staying with me, Isabelle was surprised to receive a telephone call from Guy Roux. Anxious about his players, the manager of Auxerre wanted to find out about the strength of our relationship. Events were going to show me that this action was not ill intentioned. On the contrary.

He was going to send me to my girlfriend knowing quite well that I would not live in Martigues but would spend my time in Aix-en-Provence, just a few miles away. Guy Roux wanted me, quite simply, to live on love and fresh air for several months.

I didn't need any persuading. A telephone call to Isabelle was enough. A week after Guy Roux had made the suggestion, I was loading my old Peugeot 104 to go off to Aix-en-Provence. And when I say loading, that's an understatement. I had emptied my flat of everything – clothes, books, television. Everything was put into the 104. And it's not easy to fit a huge black and white television set in the passenger's seat. Jammed up against the steering wheel, I couldn't see anything in my mirrors and the most disturbing factor in all this was that I had passed my driving test only six weeks previously and here I was getting ready to spend several hours behind the wheel in this state. My mother had phoned me earlier and she wasn't wrong in recommending prudence. But there was little chance of that the way I was feeling.

I needed only a couple of days to leave everything – Auxerre, the manager, Nino, that town which gave me my first experience as an apprentice pro – but Isabelle and I had said too much, exchanged too many ideas and too many feelings not to be sure of ourselves.

Isabelle occupied a small studio in Aix-en-Provence, having only just finished her studies. In fact, it was so tiny that we tended to get in each other's way.

The day after my arrival I signed a loan contract tying me to Martigues until the end of the season. We were not rolling in money but we enjoyed our lives, without doubt because we were happy with simple pleasures. I remember causing quite a stir after one interview when I said that money didn't make happiness. These days, to many people, that seems a strange thing to say, but it is how I feel.

Money has not changed my life and it will never change it. Perhaps you may find it odd that I should think that happiness does not come from being able to buy a car that one wants or in having money which has been saved in a bank account. I don't. It's all a matter of upbringing. My brothers and I were never given many presents. My parents weren't rich enough to rush off to the shops, but it was also a matter of choice on their part.

As a child I wanted to be a diver. But I cannot count the number of plastic bottles that I tied to my back to help me enjoy my hobby. On the shore near the family home I had no doubt that I had the best diving bottles in all the world. I can't remember ever having been given a bow and arrow. With Jean-Marie and Joël we discovered that there were plenty of them in the forests and that there was no need to ask for such a toy. The woods are full of bows and arrows. It was simply a matter of making them, and they always seemed so much better for that reason.

In Martigues we were obviously very careful with our money. But it was also a time when we discovered the countryside and places of interest. With the help of a map which we unfolded in the middle of our room, it was quite easy to choose a village, a hill, somewhere deep in the country, and set off there. With Isabelle I enjoyed the Camargue, its horses, Saintes-Maries-de-la-Mer. We also visited the picturesque village of les Baux in Provence. And we danced at the Nice carnival. In these quiet places we were able to rest and relax and enjoy each other's company.

I had almost forgotten about football. Guy Roux was now merely someone in the distance. My parents began to get worried. My father would have liked it if I had given some news to Guy Roux to let him know how my career was going. I told him that my mind was elsewhere. For the first time in my life, I was sharing things with a lovely girl of 22 years of age. I was 19 and the world could have crumbled at our door.

Football hadn't died in me but it was drowsing dangerously.

Guy Roux woke me up. I was going to sign, at the age of 20, my first professional contract. One evening in June 1986, he was in the stands of Gerland stadium, the home of Lyon. Martigues were playing Lyon, who were hoping to win promotion to the first division. After the match he met my father in the corridors and confided in him that he had made up his mind: 'Your son will be playing for Auxerre next season.'

It was a double challenge: first, it was an attempt to put the formidable years of Szarmach behind the club so we could move on, and second it gave me the chance to play as quickly as possible after nine months relaxing in the second division. The stakes were high but this time I wasn't alone, as Guy Roux well knew.

I was returning with the woman of my life.

Sometimes your life can be changed within a few months. I left Auxerre not being able to know if I would ever come back to the Abbé Deschamps stadium. But now that day had arrived at last. My time away from Auxerre had put my career back on course.

A top-level sportsman needs to find his equilibrium outside the football ground or the running track or the jumping pits. Nobody has the right to make a judgement on what they do away from their sport. Jacques Anquetil, one of the greatest cyclists in the history of that sport, could allow himself to play poker or drink

Playing for Auxerre against Paris St Germain in August 1986, aged 20. (Presse-Sports)

champagne the night before a very important mountain stage. But, even if his health was undoubtedly affected by that, it didn't stop him winning five Tours de France between 1957 and 1964. And above all, he gave millions of spectators the opportunity to dream on the side of the roads. Maradona took cocaine far from the stadium of San Paolo where he was a god every Sunday afternoon. And I consider that a legal system, whether it's in Italy or Argentina, is nevertheless not in a position to give lessons of virtue and morality to anybody.

Maradona should never have been suspended from the game that he had graced for so long. When you are not playing football, or running, or boxing, or when you leave the tennis courts it's your right to live as you want to do.

At Auxerre I was free. I was free again to put cartridges in my gun and go and hunt woodcock and pigeons after training. I was at liberty to begin a session of psychoanalysis without being called a madman. I was free to paint and to live 20 kilometres from Auxerre with my Isabelle and my dogs. And it was in this period of time that I made the majority of friends that I have kept until this day. Glory often coincides with the development of what turn out to be very superficial relationships. Anyone who has not got any solid foundations before achieving celebrity often finds himself alone when he ceases to be famous. In Yonne with Isabelle, we tasted marvellous moments of tranquillity.

The silence of the countryside has always been indispensable for me. The calm of nature precedes and follows excitement at the stadiums. I have always needed such a contrast. Wherever my clubs have been, I have always tried to maintain this lifestyle.

At Auxerre, I spent some unforgettable moments playing football on Saturday evening and some marvellous times of solitude and friendship the rest of the week.

It was also the time for experiments.

The management of Auxerre had taken us off to Roscoff two days before playing against Brest in the championship. We had a hotel reserved for us by the sea and had brought along our own hairdresser. That evening I wanted to have my head shaved and to feel the fresh rain and the strength of the wind on my skull, so by five in the afternoon on the eve of the match I didn't have a hair on my head. Guy Roux was worried about what Isabelle would think about it and he phoned to tell her the news.

'What are you saying "he has shaven his head"? But what do you mean, "shaved"?' she asked.

'Like an egg, Isabelle, like an egg. Just like an egg,' Guy Roux replied.

For my pals – Nino Ferrer, Prunier, Dutuel – my bullet head had no effect

Cantona has always craved the freedom and tranquillity of the countryside. (Presse-Sports/Colorsport)

on them. Nothing changed the training, our desire to win, our ambition. And they also had a spark of impertinence and insolence in their eyes.

But for the press, they had the impression that they had discovered the Yeti of Burgundy, and I began to get worried. Hunter, painter, brazen...and bald at 20.

For Isabelle, however, it was a bit of a joke. It was late in the night when we returned from Brest. I had to slide into bed. She stroked the top of my head and realised with some amazement that I didn't have the semblance of a hair on my head. Guy Roux had not been joking.

It was around this time that Cantona first gained international recognition, playing for the French Under-21 side in their European Championship competition. As in Euro 96, Cantona was not to be there at the climax, but to this day he remembers the marvellous team spirit of that side:

Performances at club level influence selection for the national side.

With the Under-21 team we had a group of players who were ready to take on and destroy all-comers. On 12 October 1988 in Besançon we beat Greece 3-0 to become champions of Europe. But this was done without me, because in the meantime I had made some remarks about the national team manager, Henri Michel, which caused me to be suspended from all international matches for a year. The tearaway had been deprived of his desserts. But I'll come back to that later.

It was a fabulous saga of the Under-21 team. Canal+, the satellite station, was

Guy Roux described Cantona's shaven head as 'just like an egg'. (Colorsport)

Playing for the French Under-21 side against England at Highbury in the 1988 European Championship semi-final. (Colorsport)

wise enough to retransmit our epic games, and so brought us great publicity. Nothing was ever to be the same again for the players. The history of this group of turbulent young footballers began in Le Havre in October 1986. The Soviets still had an international team; Gorbachev was in the Kremlin. They were the favourites in our group but we were able to beat them in Normandy. A clap of thunder: we won 2-1. I scored both goals.

The remarkable story of the Under-21 team had begun with that surprise victory. But it was in England at Highbury in the second leg of the semi-final that brought us our most marvellous memories.

Two days before the crunch match at Highbury I had decided that the time had come to leave Auxerre. The press ran the story with the following headline on the morning of the match: 'Cantona about to depart'. With such a fanfare it was necessary to succeed in my examination in England and show those watching that I would be a good signing. In front of the cameras of Canal+, which was transmitting the game live from England, I had a marvellous game.

The important events of a career are sometimes accompanied by lighthearted anecdotes. The traffic was frightful thanks to the British weather and nearly cost us the match. The coach that took us to the stadium arrived just three-quarters of an hour before the kick-off. You can think of better conditions in which to play an international match. It rained at Highbury. The stadium, covered by a mist, was simply a battlefield. Who knows if the 22 soldiers lost in the mêlée heard the cheers of the spectators?

For us it wasn't important. Stéphane Paille and I combined together marvellously. Twice he gave me a ball with his back to the opponent's defence. It paid off.

After our win 4-2 in the home match, this 2-2 drawn match in England enabled us to qualify for the final. The press didn't take long in making heroes of us. For me the voyage didn't stop there.

The reason I had just put in a transfer request was that Auxerre had just been eliminated in the quarter-final of the French Cup by Lille. I was very disappointed by this defeat. But, in the dressing room, Guy Roux tried to explain to us at length that a defeat in the last eight against Lille was not catastrophic. It was just a mistake of youth, lack of experience. But by then I was a player who had already made 80 appearances in the first division and no longer felt inexperienced. Guy Roux's explanation did not satisfy me. As a child I had dreamed too much of the French Cup to be able to endure such a disappointment. I was more ambitious than he seemed to be for the club.

I still didn't know it, but the essential things had been said and done: I had announced that I wanted to leave the club and performed well enough to ensure that there would be plenty of interest in signing me. Auxerre, at the end of the 1988 season, was behind me. I was 22 on 24 May and I already had good memories in my locker.

I had only to choose my destination. Stupid people are convinced that a footballer goes only where the money is. If they don't want to die as idiots they should know that there are other things which also form part of negotiations. That said, in a set-up which can generate huge sums it's reasonable that the principal actors of the show ask for their share.

By the age of 22, Cantona had already played five times for France and he was attracting the attention of bigger clubs than Auxerre, among them his home-town club of Olympique Marseille.

The summer of 1988 is approaching. The last weeks have been spent in Burgundy.

I had now played for Auxerre, the Under-21s and made my debut for the French national team. In my first match, I had scored France's only goal in Berlin in a 2-1 defeat against West Germany on 12 August 1987 – it was, on a personal level, a great start and it was followed by other good signs. I had become a media personality and their interest increased as we entered into the period of transfers.

Cantona hits one
on the volley for
France against
Cyprus in the
World Cup
qualifier on 18
November 1989.
(*Presse-Sports*)

Another
spectacular volley -
this time for Leeds
United against
Aston Villa in
August 1992.
(*Presse-Sports*)

'I was eight when I first discovered all the shades and colours of the universe in my father's workshop.' (*Colorsport*)

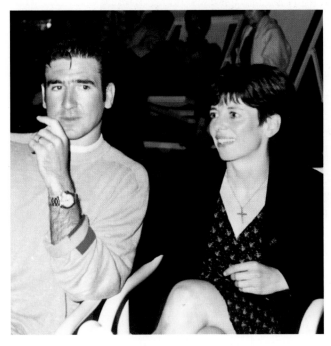

On holiday with Isabelle.

Opposite Modelling for Paco Rabanne – an interesting experience for Cantona, but not a new career. (*Empics*)

'The penalty is either happiness or sadness, nothing in between.' The moment of truth, France v Sweden, 28 April 1993. (*P. Boutroux/Presse-Sports*)

Cantona, penalty-taker supreme, sets up a 2–1 victory for the French. The USA was in their sights – but it was not to be. (*P. Boutroux/Presse-Sports*)

Cantona likes to entertain – in more ways than one.

Charity Shield, 8 August 1992: Cantona lets fly, beating the Liverpool defence . . . (*Popperfoto*)

. . . and goalkeeper Bruce Grobbelaar to score Leeds' third – and his second – goal in their 4–3 triumph. (*Empics*)

European Cup first round, second leg: Cantona scores Leeds' third goal in their 4–1 win over Stuttgart. (*Popperfoto*)

Cantona with his son Raphaël, aged four, at Old Trafford. Manchester United legend Bobby Charlton is in the foreground on the left.

Wearing the red shirt of United. Cantona was immediately in the thick of things at his new club. (*Presse-Sports*)

He makes his debut in the new colours against derby rivals Manchester City in December 1992.(*Empics*)

Cantona, the media personality. (Empics)

One of my best friends in the Auxerre team, Pascal Planques, had advised me to find a good agent. At 22 years of age it's not very easy to find one's way in the labyrinth of financial negotiations. I had to rely on a person who is used to the practices necessary in such dealings. Pascal pointed me in the direction of his own agent, Alain Migliaccio.

He very quickly understood what I wanted. I was going to place my interests in the hands of a man whose job it was to organise transfers. My travels have made him do some spectacular pirouettes. Since that time we have gone our separate ways, but I have never had occasion to complain about the route which we took together.

From the beginning of June 1988, Alain Migliaccio knew the name of clubs who were interested in signing me. Looking through the offers, we were able to eliminate quite easily those clubs in which we had no interest. There was one certainty: I would not be going to Italy. I did not feel ready to confront the Italian style of football with its rigid defences.

As we formed a more precise impression of the offers, both in financial and sporting terms, it was clear that there were two front-runners: Marseille and Matra-Racing, a club formed by the Matra company.

I had three weeks in which to make my choice. I had to decide whether I wanted to return to my youth, my family, my town, or to say yes to a club with a growing reputation. This decision was sufficiently difficult for me that I felt that I had to speak with my psychoanalyst. I had started seeing him because of my interest in the subconscious and, like many others in France, found that my sessions with him were very useful. It wasn't a question of being worried about my state of mind. These sessions of analysis, which I had started with him several months before, were now sufficiently advanced for him to be able to predict my future. He advised me not to sign for Marseille but recommended that I should go to England, which wasn't a bad prediction when you think of it. He wasn't judging a club: he was looking only at the well-being of his patient.

Since 1984, Olympique Marseille had rediscovered its fame and the club's ground, boulevard Michelet, had found its dignity. That year I had paid a lot of attention to the exploits of the young Marseille players who had helped the club to get back into the first division after four long years in purgatory.

Bernard Tapie had taken control of the club in 1986. With the manager Michel Hidalgo and the trainer Gérard Banide, Olympique Marseille were intent on rediscovering the magic of the years of Skoblar and Magnusson. On 20 October 1971, perched on the shoulders of my father, I had been among the 48,000 spectators in the Vélodrome at the crunch match of the year: Olympique Marseille against Ajax in the second round of the European Cup. Ajax, who were the Cup holders, went on to retain the trophy.

Seventeen years later, Tapie had given me the opportunity to rediscover the same emotions, playing with Marseille. It was difficult to decline his offer.

Gérard Banide had come to see me at Auxerre. We had mainly spoken about tactics, as the OM trainer saw me in the position of playmaker.

The tug of war which went on between Olympique Marseille and Matra-Racing was, however, far from being ended. At the invitation of the president of the Parisian club, Jean-Luc Lagardère, I went to see him. The negotiations picked up pace.

It's certain that the unexpected visit of Bernard Tapie to see me in Burgundy had greatly contributed to my being drawn closer to Marseille. However, my decision had still not been taken. It was no longer a question of money. For several weeks my agent, Alain Migliaccio, knew what both the clubs were able to offer. There was one thing certain: I was going to multiply my salary by 20 times. The money was there in the contract. I had no reason for refusing it.

In school my teacher used to give me a star in exchange for getting ten out of ten in a test. In the same way, I considered this money to be a reward, especially as it was coming from an industrialist who uses football for his own purposes and to gain fame.

Jean-Luc Lagardère that evening hadn't just come on a whim to talk about the weather and other trivialities. He was anxious to explain his plans clearly to me, and had preferred to invite me to dinner with him at his house. For a little over three hours he explained what he was expecting from me. I had been impressed by his very accurate knowledge of the way I played. He seemed to me to be the man to bring a better organisation to Matra-Racing. He wanted to play me alongside his star attacker, the Uruguayan Enzo Francescoli, whose extraordinary touch on the ball I had admired for a long time.

It's a strange thing that I would never manage to play alongside him. Enzo suffered unfortunately from repeated pulled muscles and was also disappointed by the results of Matra and was soon transferred to Marseille. At that time, I had left the old port for Bordeaux and then Montpellier and, when I finally came back to the Vélodrome stadium, Enzo Francescoli had been transferred by Tapie.

On arriving at my host's house, I went into his living room and saw a famous painting by the Catalan painter Miró. Miró is one of my favourite painters! I didn't even dare think that the picture that I saw at Jean-Luc Lagardère's house was an original. A man of taste and culture, Lagardère presented me with two books on the subject of Picasso and Miró, respectively. I had in my hands one of the numerous reproductions, while above my head was the original.

On the pavement before climbing into the taxi, I tried to clear my head. It was about time. My choice had to be made the following morning at 11.30 and I still didn't know which one to go for. I was torn between the call of my home town and the mad desire to wager on the future success of Matra. In the hotel bar I bumped into Alain Migliaccio. I told him about my disarray. Jean-Luc Lagardère's strength of conviction had somehow, without my knowing it, distanced me from the lights of the Vélodrome. Migliaccio advised me to go and rest. I could sleep on it.

In the morning, I was a Marseillais.

Alain Migliaccio immediately telephoned Jean-Pierre Bernès, the commercial manager at Marseille who was involved in the club's transfers, and Bernard Tapie was waiting for us the same morning in his private hotel in the centre of the 16th arrondissement in order to sign the contract. At the agreed hour I had my pen in my hand, ready to sign all the pages of the contract, when the telephone, which is constantly ringing in the office of the president of Olympique Marseille, rang out again. This time it was for me. Alain's secretary had an urgent message to communicate to him. AC Milan had begun to show an interest in me. A contact of Silvio Berlusconi, the renowned president of AC Milan, wanted to meet me.

In June 1988 the club was at the dawn of its royal conquest. The players of Berlusconi were going to rule European football. On 24 May 1989 in the Nou Camp, the legendary stadium of Barcelona, before 96,000 spectators, AC Milan hammered Steaua Bucharest 4-0 in the final of the European Cup. Van Basten, Gullit, Rijkaard and Baresi had become the new masters of the round ball.

In the rooms of the Marseille president, just for a brief moment, I felt ill-at-ease learning about this interest from Milan.

'What are you going to do?' Jean-Pierre Bernès asked me.

'What am I going to do? I am signing for Marseille and that's that!'

I had come back to the club of my childhood. With such a contract I was also doing good business. But there was no danger of that going to my head. I had had the good fortune to meet a young lady whose interests were not obsessed by show and flash. Isabelle had always preferred books to sports cars. She wouldn't let me lose my values and, besides, I was no longer thinking about money because I had become the proprietor of quite another fortune and that was the possibility of wearing the white shirt of Olympique Marseille.

The Vélodrome was waiting for Cantona.

Chapter Four

· ·

Troubles

Throughout his career, Cantona has been a controversial character and he has been at the centre of many notorious incidents. He recalls those events that gave him the reputation as the enfant terrible of French football:

'I will never play for France again as long as Henri Michel is manager. Don't speak any more about him. It's a choice between Michel and myself. I would like it to be known that I think he is one of the most incompetent managers in world football. I am not far from thinking that he is a shitbag.'

These words, uttered on 20 August 1988, were, I freely admit, a true declaration of war and this declaration was all the more audacious in that it put a player of 22 years old at odds with the manager of the French national side.

Controversial Cantona: he earned a reputation as the enfant terrible *of French football.* (Empics)

However, I am not as bad as you may have been led to think. Don't believe all those images which are painted of me and made up by the media. Don't trust the rumours or the words which are misinterpreted almost as soon as they have left my mouth. You have learned to love me or leave me, depending on how you look at what has happened. In that case, I had better make clear what really did go on, as so many of these stories about my career in France have followed me to England – inevitably being further distorted.

The most ridiculous story, however, concerns the events that took place at the end of the 1989 season.

In Bordeaux, Claude Bez and his assistant, Didier Couécou, were in control at Château Hailla, the luxurious headquarters of the club. One morning, just before leaving for training, I saw my dog, Balrine, stretched out on the terrace at home. She was making a horrible and piteous whimpering noise – it was like a cry for help. She had just had a heart attack, I later learned. In a panic I went to call a vet. But unfortunately, it was a bank holiday. I was shattered by this sight of such suffering. Only animal lovers would understand how I felt at the loss of this close companion, who had been with me for two years. I missed training and returned to the club only at the beginning of the afternoon.

Much later, when I was with Montpellier, the president of that club, Louis Nicollin, several hours after having signed me, had a friendly chat with me. There was nonetheless an anxious look in his eye.

'Tell me, Eric. You don't have the intention of skipping training sessions, do you?'

I wanted to excuse that question on the basis that organising a complex transfer deal must have been very tiring and stressful. So I had to be understanding. The double transfer of Cantona and Stéphane Paille to Montpellier had been too explosive not to have had some effect on the nerves of the president. I pretended to be surprised:

'You're joking aren't you, President?'

'No, not at all. At Bordeaux, Didier Couécou told me to be on guard against your acts of truancy.'

In Bordeaux I had in fact missed only one training session: the morning of the death of my dog. So you can see what harm malice and telling tales can do – I had gained a bad reputation, that had been passed on to other clubs, on the basis of one incident.

I don't have any regrets about what I did and, if I had to do everything again tomorrow, I would do the same thing. He who has regrets cannot look at himself in the mirror. If he lets other people down, above all he knows he is letting himself down.

When you get older it doesn't mean that you have to betray your youth and its inclination to excesses. I have certainly changed: I wouldn't use the same words again about Henri Michel, but I would still be just as much against him as I was previously. I would even have a fight once again with Jean-Claude Lemoult if that was necessary. (You can read *that* story later on in this chapter.) And together, I'm sure, there would be nothing to stop us from winning another French Cup. I would never have any respect for Raymond Goethals, the manager of Marseille, because he never had any respect for his players. And I will always maintain that I met a real gentleman in the person of Franz Beckenbauer when he was at Olympique Marseille, and the same goes for Michel Platini.

And so, with complete honesty, I will relive those events in order to try to seek some kind of explanation as to why I have gained a reputation as being trouble or being difficult. And, in a little more than ten years of professional football, such incidents are not very numerous, whatever people may want to believe.

Perhaps the most controversial incident came in the summer of 1988 when I had been playing for the French national team for over a year and also for the Under-21 side. But the story begins a year before.

On 12 August 1987 the French team arrived in Berlin, where the wall was still standing, but we faltered and West Germany won 2-1. However, it was

then that I scored my first international goal in the French shirt on my full international debut. Soon after this, people began to say and write that France had at last found the attacker that the team had been missing.

However, with the Under-21 team and our manager Marc Bourrier, the champagne was flowing in the showers while the full international team led by Henri Michel was having problems. On 14 October 1987, Norway held us to a 1-1 draw in the Parc des Princes. The contrast between the two sides seemed great at that time.

Cantona has scored 20 goals for his country. Here he celebrates scoring against West Germany, the team against whom he scored his first international goal in August 1987. (Presse-Sports)

Some weeks later, on 18 November, the East German side arrived and gave us a good beating, 1-0. In front of 26,000 spectators we had lost the last qualifying match for Europe. France would not be going to Germany to take part in the European Nations Championship. Soon, we would also be out of the World Cup.

With the Under-21 side, everything was different. We were crushing all our opponents at every outing without any effort. Youth is insolent, especially when it feels it's irresistible. When I went to play for the full national side, I wish I could have taken with me all that *joie de vivre* that we had in our squad which was headed by that typical southerner, the warm and enthusiastic Marc Bourrier.

Henri Michel, who was the playmaker for the great Nantes team in the 1960s, was a marvellous player but in my opinion a bad manager. Somebody in charge, in whatever type of activity, must be able to take the pressure and the responsibilities however painful the criticism may be. In less than two years, Henri Michel had tried all of 50 players. In my opinion, it seemed that he was allowing himself to be influenced too much by the commentaries of the sporting press about the composition of the team.

When you don't know you are afraid.

And then I cracked. I said, as always, precisely what I thought without in any way holding back. My team-mates thought the same as I did but didn't have the courage to say things which could knock them off the route that had been marked out for them since their childhood. In the special football schools, as in army training camps, the key words are simple and straightforward: don't ask questions! Many of my team-mates had remembered that lesson. I must have forgotten it.

In the months before my outburst things had gone very well for me on a personal level. On 23 March 1988 in Bordeaux we won 2-1 against Spain. For the previous two seasons our performances had been poor and our spectators had gone away disappointed. This victory at the expense of Spain, even though it was a friendly match, had the feel of a revival and rebirth. Goals by Passi and Luis Fernandez had seen us home. I felt well; I love victory.

However, the celebrations were only just beginning. A month later, in Greece with the Under-21 team in the away leg in the final of the European Championship, we managed a very encouraging 1-1 draw which put us in with an excellent chance of victory in the return match at home.

The French team of the future is alive and kicking.

Olympique Marseille had bought me during the summer break for the sum of 22 million francs (then worth about £2.3 million). I found myself immediately in the spotlight of French football; I didn't have room for error nor the time to adapt to my new team. After five matches in my new colours, I still hadn't scored a goal even though I may have made some.

On 17 August 1988 I scored my first goal for Marseille against Matra-Racing, the club I had so nearly joined. On the next morning, the national team manager announced the names of 16 players for the game against Czechoslovakia in the Parc des Princes. I was not among those chosen. 'Eric is not on his best form,' commented Henri Michel. After what had gone before, this was a huge disappointment.

So, on Saturday 20 August 1988, while still not at my best form, I scored another goal against Strasbourg in a match where everything went right for me. We won 3-2 in front of 40,000 spectators and after the match I exploded.

Lights, sound, action! The camera turns and in the dressing rooms of Strasbourg there is suddenly a scoop. 'Canto' loses his rag and calls the national manager a 'shitbag'. A fine kettle of fish!

Very quickly I became afraid. I had been trapped by my own words. But the public at large that evening remembered only a picture of a young man who was emotionally disturbed. Worse, without doubt, they thought. On seeing myself a little later on the television screen and in the newspapers I was afraid. A gloomy face invaded the screen, and for the viewer his words were punctuated by the term 'shitbag'.

The public is not wicked. It doesn't believe all that it sees, but what it had seen this time had made it afraid. I hadn't told any lies but I had been clumsy. I needed to learn the art of communication. The history of French football will remember that I had prepared the ground for others in no uncertain manner.

I was like a fuse wire. Once I had been lit, the explosion which followed would ensure that the misery of the French national team could be ended and we could begin rebuilding. I had publicly apologised for my remarks and I had tried to explain the situation to Henri Michel. A ban, however, was going to be imposed. On 9 September, in the evening, I was officially excluded from selection for national teams for a period of a year. I was prevented from playing five full international matches. I would not participate in the return final match of the Under-21 European Championship against Greece.

On 22 October in Nicosia, the French national team drew 1-1 against Cyprus. The result was a humiliation and heads rolled – Henri Michel was the first. He was to be succeeded by Michel Platini.

Three months had passed since my outburst in Strasbourg. I thought that all I had done was to say some stupid things. I comforted my friends by telling them that I would put matters right the next time, but I let my enemies know that I had no intention of changing my ways. A young man has a right to rebel. I had lit the wick and battle had commenced. Many people took the opportunity of shooting at me.

In the end it was of little importance. Henri Michel had to leave and he went.

'A player who throws his shirt on the ground, even if he has scored three goals in the match, must be sanctioned because that's not what we expect from sport. This doesn't correspond to the idea which I have of football in general and of football at Olympique Marseille in particular.'

These strong words were spoken on 30 January 1989 by, you could well guess, Bernard Tapie. It is true that his way of looking at football is the opposite of mine. Recent events have proved, to those who had any doubts about it, that his noble ideas do accommodate less honourable behaviour, at least in relation to what constitutes in my eyes the *raison d'être* of sport.

In any case, I had discovered, in the course of a friendly match between Olympique Marseille and Torpedo Moscow, in aid of the Armenian Disaster Fund, in Sedan the devastating power a single image can create. I merely had to throw my shirt on the ground that day for my future at Marseille to be put in doubt. Before me, the English player Laurie Cunningham had dared to do the same thing.

Then it had been at the Vélodrome stadium on 14 May 1985, Marseille were playing Lens and needed to win to ensure that they stayed up in the premier division. Early in the game Cunningham was replaced by Eric Di Meco. He was very upset by that and threw his shirt onto the grass. This act was greeted by whistles from the public.

At Sedan, a local but smaller ground than the Vélodrome, the cameras were rolling, but the only image that is transmitted shows a bare-chested player making his way to the dressing rooms.

Each time that I see my puppet on the television show that is the French equivalent to *Spitting Image*, it is always that gesture of irritation which comes to the screen the most often. It's funny. I like Picasso, as my character is named (because of my interest in art), and I think that what he does and says in the studio does no harm to anyone. 'Ah! But what about the importance of setting an example for the young people?' you say to me. My reply to that is that I think one should stop treating the heart and soul of youngsters as clay to be modelled in whatever fashion you like. I am not there to educate anyone; I don't see that as my role. They should be able to work things out for themselves.

Children go where they find sincerity and authenticity. In my way of working, of carrying out my career, I don't betray anybody and they know it. I don't consider that it would be better to teach them to deny their own emotions for the benefit of the established order. Is it in teaching people to be submissive that they become adult citizens?

At Sedan, as later at Nîmes, I wanted to tell the public that they were being cheated, because I was being set up as a scapegoat by the management. It was too easy to set me up in the firing line.

Inevitably, the press also joined in with the attack, as can be witnessed for example by the comments of the journalist Denis Chaumier in *l'Equipe*: 'By his gesture, Cantona has practically scuppered himself.' The public was given just one side of the story.

Those remarks were not helpful and my best reply comes in the fact that the ship is still sailing. In reality, this gesture was a natural part of my personality. I take responsibility for it. There are perhaps more beautiful or more ugly personalities. The great feature of someone who wants to please at any price is his capacity for hiding from the public certain things which should be condemned. You need a particular talent only to want to please. I don't have this talent.

What makes it worse for such critics is that I have an enormous fault: I don't attach any importance to what people say about me at my expense. What does me a lot of good comes from within myself, from the conviction that I have played a good match, and not from what others say. It's incredible but there are some players who prefer to read their name mentioned by error as having scored a goal on Saturday afternoon in the league championship rather than having scored a goal without anybody knowing about it.

I shall never renounce the kind of relationship I have with the public, the press and the television. If I hadn't had the strength of character to take responsibility for my mouthing off, in ten years of my career I would have sunk. Nobody would have come to fish me out. I leave it to politicians and to our managers to be sufficiently smooth to disguise all of their emotions. I do not see that I should follow their lead.

I must admit that I am not displeased by the fact that I was suspended by a man whose operations are being shown by the system of justice to rest on lies and trickery. The president of Olympique Marseille, three days after the incident in Sedan, threatened to send me to a clinic. God be praised that I escaped the straitjacket! The club later saw their error because Marseille, after my performance for Montpellier which helped them to victory in the French Cup in June 1990, came back for me.

By throwing away my shirt, I was wrong. But only in terms of the image it created of me and in terms of my career.

In over eight years of marriage to Isabelle, it seems to me that we have never abandoned certain values. I have earned the right to hold my head up high. And once again it was the family, my own people, who helped me and understood me.

I decided to go to Barcelona to stay with my friend Michel Pinéda, who plays for Santander in the Spanish first division, after I had been suspended for throwing down my shirt. The air of the Ramblas did me a lot of good. The Catalan nights were beautiful at that time and my meetings with my grandfather Pedro helped to put my thoughts in order. It had been several months since I had last seen him. It was only by listening to the radio that he had understood about my difficulties. A well-fulfilled life had given him a good sense of humour. My grandfather just told me to be a little bit more prudent.

Two weeks later I was packing my bags for Bordeaux. I was loaned to the Girondins until the end of the championship. The sadness of having failed, at least provisionally, at Marseille did not give rise to any regrets. In the Marseille squad which I was leaving, the players had all forgotten about the shirt that I had thrown down and didn't hold anything against me.

I think this stands as proof that among that group of people I had never sought to impose my ideas. I have never wanted everybody to think as I do. I asked only for a little respect to be given to my ideas. The world of sport has changed. Football has become such a political and commercial game that it has become too powerful for its actors – the players – to have the right to speak. It so happened that I had committed the cardinal sin of speaking out, and if I happened to have made some mistakes in precisely what I had said, at least I had the courage to stick to the end with the spirit of what I had said.

I now realise that it wasn't the jersey that I threw down which upset people but it was the person who threw it. And the insults I made about Henri Michel don't weigh so heavily on me nowadays, because I now know about the plot to remove him of which he was a victim some weeks later.

Edouard Münch, the early 20th-century painter, never ceased modifying his work depending on his moods. He was an honest man. Similarly, who can claim to get up each morning in the same frame of mind?

That is why I admire artists so much: they are pledged to move our emotions and they are accountable only to themselves. They don't have the right to trick anybody because they are soon shown up.

In the world of football, there are very few athletes who have that feel of immortality: Pelé, Maradona, Platini. The images of them are so powerful that the very mention of their names is enough to recall their performances. As for myself, not wishing to sound immodest, I shall be delighted if my goals for France and my goals for Manchester United give you something to dream about. Nothing else is important.

As for myself, I still believed in Marseille. I had signed for the club because it has the ability to move those who live nearby to passion on the evenings of the match. So what if Bernard Tapie no longer liked me? Let him be reassured, I no longer liked him.

Jean Tigana was waiting for me when my plane landed at Bordeaux-Mérignac airport. The children of the Caillols always finish up discovering each other. We made our way to the Novotel. Sleep.

One day, I knew for certain, I would come back to Marseille.

'To condemn a person for the sole reason that he is different bears but one name: intolerance.' Michel Nait-Challal. *L'Equipe*, 26/10/1989.

At Montpellier I had a fight in the dressing room with my team-mate Jean-Claude Lemoult. I was assassinated by the press, threatened with dismissal by my club and then brought back into the side in order to finish as French Cup-winners. What a season!

The summer of 1989 had begun thus: two footballers, two friends who had dreamed of playing together for a long time, were at last reunited under the same colours: Paille and Cantona at Montpellier. Behind the term 'oneness' there are many emotions. I was rediscovering a brother by moving some 80 miles west along the coast from Marseille.

The club and the town of Montpellier were thirsting for glory. Montpellier-la-Paillade was dead. We would henceforth have to say Montpellier-Hérault, as the town was renamed. There were a lot of people on 16 July 1989 surrounding the president of the club, Louis Nicollin, when the contracts were signed. Stéphane Paille and I were happy. It was a simple happiness. We wanted to do good things together in front of the fervent spectators of the Mosson stadium.

I had agreed to reduce my salary by half in order to play with Stéphane. The sum was far less than what would accrue to the club and to the town and to the region by the presence of our two names on the football field. He had come from Sochaux. By spending so much on us Louis Nicollin had placed a terrible amount of pressure on his own shoulders.

However, in the shadow of this double transfer, a certain bitterness began to develop. It was simmering under the surface at first, but then became apparent a few weeks later.

In Lille, on the evening of a defeat, the tension blew up. It is worth remembering that even before my fight with Jean-Claude Lemoult there was no longer any question of Montpellier getting a place in Europe at the end of the season. We were occupying only a middle position in the league. Instead, it was really a matter of saving the club from possible demotion into the second division. Montpellier, having finished just in the top half of the division the year before, held dreams of glory which were well advertised at the beginning of the 1989–90 season. But it had all turned into a nightmare. There were sour looks on the faces of the sponsors, anxiety among the club management, a feverish mood in the town, backed by its mayor and his assistants. The euphoria of success sometimes allows you to forget the small hatreds which accumulate quite naturally among a group of men. It is only in defeat and adversity that you can measure the stability of a club.

Many believed that the reason Montpellier was sinking was because of Stéphane and me. The club reached rock bottom on Saturday 27 September 1989. We were playing at Lille and the defeat was the last straw.

The beautiful pattern that Louis Nicollin and Aimé Jacquet, the manager, had imagined they could create had looked all right on paper, but the management of Montpellier had worked without any safety net. They had expected a balanced team to develop in the space of a few weeks between old and new players. Our mission was to interpret *The Magic Flute* every Saturday at the Mosson stadium. Thrills and goals in perfect harmony.

Such high expectations were a mistake.

At the final whistle on this particular Saturday evening, it was a wounded group of people who went back to the dressing rooms of the Lille stadium. In the corridor Jean-Claude Lemoult murmured something to Der Sakarian – which I understood to mean that the attackers, that is Stéphane and myself, were not up to it. It was a time of whispering campaigns. The arrow hit its target. It's too late now for me to try to explain. I threw my boots into the face of Lemoult. Jean-Claude replied in kind. Inside the dressing room the fight passed off like lightning. The door opens, it's finished. But I had already been punished. Excluded. Within a few hours, on the radio and in the newspapers, publicity is given to this new 'Cantona affair'.

Later on, Louis Nicollin regretted his earlier decision to do nothing. His action against me was designed merely to cause a stir rather than treating the disease at its roots. Our team was already shipwrecked. The players were practically not speaking to each other and the bitterness had been accumulating even before I arrived.

However, it was obvious that I was going to be seen as the symbol of the failure of Montpellier-Hérault.

I was 23 years old and already there had been several complaints and reproaches about me. I had insulted the national team manager, thrown down a jersey at Marseille. And what else had there been? An evening with the American actor Mickey Rourke, who I admired for his independence and rebelliousness. I had also admitted to warm feelings for Isabelle Adjani, because of her ability to play difficult and complex roles in films such as *Subway* and *Camille Claudel*. I had admired her for being her own person – in contrast to the TV reporter Patrick Sabatier, who struck me as a yes-man. The press, needless to say, leapt upon this story. There was also my passion for bullfighting, and my hatred of injustice. For I appreciate those who are non-conventional and original – they can give so much more.

To tell you the truth, I will never be able to say how courageous Jean-Claude Lemoult was. I admit that I provoked him in the dressing rooms at Lille and he replied. We fought. But, nine months later, in the Parc des Princes, we carried off the French Cup together, winning 2-1 against Matra-Racing.

Louis Nicollin had suspended me from all activity within the club afterwards. I was finally brought back into the team ten days later. It was true that half a dozen players had signed a petition against me, but after a week the stands of la Mosson were shouting my name. Stéphane Paille was not the only player in the team to give me his support. Alongside him were Julio César, Nono, Suvrijn, Laurent Blanc and Carlos Valderama.

As the days passed, the management of Montpellier could see that a brief exchange of blows in the dressing room had done a lot of good for everybody, as long as it was now forgotten. Like a thunderstorm, it had cleared the air.

By the end of the week, Jean-Claude had forgotten about our quarrel and refused to howl with the wolves. One way or another, it seemed, we had said everything. A page had just been turned. We had needed days and even weeks of incomprehension to arrive at these extremes.

On Wednesday 1 November I took part in the training sessions again.

And then, perhaps by chance, we began to play better, as if liberated from an insupportable weight. The sporting sensation of the year was soon going to take place. Our place in the first division was now safe. There still remained the French Cup to play for and one can always dream of winning it. I played the matches in May and June with a new spirit. I was happy to have rediscovered my best form.

That evening of 15 May 1990 as we took on Saint-Etienne, it was difficult to tell whether Louis Nicollin, who was on the bench, was streaming with sweat or whether it was the incessant rain which was drenching him and everyone else in the stadium.

At Saint-Etienne I was in my element. We were in the semi-final of the French Cup. A team which rediscovers the light after several weeks in a dungeon can be difficult to play against. We were too thirsty for victory to go down to the Saint-Etienne team. So when the ball came to me from the left, a well-weighted pass from Kader Ferhaoui, I hit a volley: 1-0.

Montpellier were through to the final of the French Cup. Jean-Claude Lemoult and I hug each other and we will meet up again later on that evening in the wine bars of Nîmes.

Two days later, at the Vélodrome stadium, Olympique Marseille was beaten by Matra-Racing 1-0 in the other semi-final. Now we had to win at the Parc des Princes in the final to get into Europe.

It's 8 June 1990 and Montpellier, still improving, is going to win the French Cup in front of 45,000 spectators. It certainly wasn't the most beautiful of finals, but it was a match full of suspense. The drama makes you forget everything else. We had to go to extra time before we achieved ultimate success, 2-1.

The Cup was ours. Montpellier could get drunk with champagne on the Champs-Elysées after the victory. And Jean-Claude Lemoult and I were able to toast each other. This success was ours: it belonged to the players and to our manager Michel Mezy, who had been able to find the words which revitalised the team.

The next day, on our return to Montpellier, thousands of supporters waited

Victory celebrations: Montpellier, winners of the French Cup in 1990, parade the trophy down the Champs-Elysées. (Presse-Sports)

for us in the Place de la Comédie to celebrate this extraordinary victory, and to look at the magnificent trophy. This gathering at last made me forget all the rest of the troubles earlier in the season.

*Cantona believes in remaining true to his dream of how football should be played –
without cheating. For others to live up to the standards of this dream has become
increasingly difficult as the pressures for success continue to grow. In his
autobiography, written before the 1994 World Cup, he reveals the truth about drug-
taking in the sport and contrasts this with Maradona's much-publicised cocaine
problems. He was later to join the Argentinian in setting up the International
Association of Professional Footballers.*

'He who doesn't know is an imbecile. But he who knows and doesn't say
anything is a criminal.' Brecht.

My book will not be a speech for the prosecution against Bernard Tapie. I
have already admitted that I don't like him as a person, but it is the system
used by people like him that I want to destroy. For, to be fair, the same system
is used by other club presidents. I leave it to others to help the officer in charge
of the investigation. They will certainly have need of more witnesses to make
any progress in their investigations. On the other hand, nobody has the
means to keep everybody quiet.

I was six years old. Each morning in the bedroom which I shared with my
brother Joël I got up early to check that my sports bag hadn't been stolen in
the night and that my studded boots were well polished. At the age of four I
played every day as I was already touched by the passion of the game. In the
streets, in the sunshine, on the club ground of the Caillols, in the fields, on the
shore, in the Spanish garden at my grandparents'… it didn't matter, I always
needed a ball.

Nobody ever made us play football or watch it, and today the game should
belong to those of us who love it. Football belongs to those who love it to such
a point that they want to make a career of it. We had a garden of paradise.
Money and cheats have trampled on it and they are still trampling on it.

My dream has been shattered.

I have been disappointed to discover that we players are only merchandise
which passes from club to club. I have seen the deceit at work and I have seen
the pills which you are advised to take in the dressing room in order to
improve your performance.

Yes, we are only expensive merchandise. Being conscious and aware of that
will help you to take part more easily in negotiations with an employer,
because you understand how you are seen.

It's not a secret to anyone that the market of products and also the market
of men don't do us any favours, and European football is now part of such a
trade. On this chessboard the players are only pawns to bring money and
fame.

Nowadays, as a club chairman or president, you often have to master other parameters than the sole concern of putting together a harmonious and efficient team. You must win at all costs, because victory means money, which also means power. Don't hesitate to threaten or bend the rules or appropriate the game in order to consolidate your own power. Because of this, we, the sportsmen, players and referees, are being used, and so is the public.

The football 'business' wasn't born in France. In France we merely imitate slavishly the methods used elsewhere, right up to the point of caricature.

I shall never get used to the spectacle of French club presidents who pretend to speak about the game better than we, the actors. They are afraid for their money, their sponsors, their image. But they would be surprised to learn that in England, for example, a president of a club would rarely dare push himself forward. The public doesn't often know the presidents: it knows the players and the managers. In England, at Leeds and at Manchester United, as well as all the other top clubs, the star people are the players. It's they who win or lose matches. It is they who make the stadiums of Elland Road, Anfield and Old Trafford vibrate. It is rarely the presidents that attract the headlines, even though they invest just as much money in the clubs as their French counterparts. When you visit the museums at clubs such as Manchester United and Liverpool, you can measure the weight of the sporting history in Great Britain and the respect which they all have for the ethics of the game. In England, the club set-ups remain true to the spirit of the sport.

As a matter of fact, I genuinely believe that a system which pushes the administrators of a club to the forefront rather than the players is in danger. The worst possible methods can be used by men without scruples.

Where there is money, there are also cheats and they both go together. I would so like it to be understood how many footballers do not play football just to make money. Similarly, it is not a rarity to meet actors in the theatre or the cinema for whom the simple deed of reading a text or interpreting a role is the most important thing. You only have to love the game in order to understand that.

With the barrage of reports and pictures which come from all over the world, the champion is often seen as a prima donna. He is a star. However, when Carl Lewis beat the world record for the 100 metres in Tokyo in the World Championship in August 1991 his tears were those of man overcome by emotion. In the Barcelona Olympic Games of 1992, when the young Ethiopian runner Derartu Tulu, winner of the 10,000 metres, left the track arm in arm with the second-placed runner, the South African Elana Meyer, the world trembled at this sign of reconciliation. When Alain Giresse beat the air of Seville with his fists on 13 June 1982 after his second goal against Germany, you can bet that this emotion was not in any way tied to the match bonus.

Only sport is capable of giving us such a treasure. But this richness should command respect. So when I speak about cheats, I think that it's indispensable to put in the same category those who want to buy victory as the champion who takes drugs to be the strongest. What good can come to a runner who cheats before the start of the 100 metres or the player who swallows amphetamine pills before the kick-off? Not much.

What I have seen in football circles in ten years of professional soccer entitles me to feel that our dream has flown away. But we must survive. As if by chance, it is those who are the most corrupt who are also the happiest to condemn Maradona. What hypocrisy! The important distinction is that Diego Maradona didn't take cocaine to be the best player on the field. His private life does not concern me. Ben Johnson used drugs to make him run faster, and so he was cheating.

International football gets rid of a player whose left foot will remain immortal while allowing, every Saturday in France, footballers greatly inferior to him to take drugs before going onto the pitch. I have never gone onto the field with the help of any kind of drug for several reasons.

A sportsman who takes drugs doesn't betray only his sport. He also destroys the trust of the public, who are fascinated by his performances. How can a footballer on drugs have the courage to look himself in the mirror in the dressing room after taking a shower, or to confront journalists, or sign autographs, or later enjoy his goals? I think that it must be very difficult to play a lie and to lie in play. As far as I am concerned, I have always refused. Wherever I have gone it's my body, my head and my eyes which have played. Even when my body has sometimes been worn out and tired, or perhaps injured as it was six months before the final of the Champions' Cup at Bari while at Marseille, it has always been clean and healthy.

One day I will explain to my son Raphaël that you can't make an apology for sport as a human activity containing so many joys while, at the same time, you give yourself a jab just as you give a shot to horses before a race. I prefer to play badly than to cheat in this way. I prefer even the whistles of the crowd, rather than the cheers for a passing train which smokes.

To cheat the spectators who have paid to see the game, to cheat the opponents, to cheat yourself – I find that impossible.

I have just one thing to say to those who are considering cheating in this way: please don't shatter our dream! In the sunshine, on the roads of Marseille, in the mist and the puddles of the built-up areas of Lens in the north, in front of the tower blocks of Aubervilliers, on the beaches of the Atlantic, in the cold of Lorraine, in the wasteland of Saint-Etienne, all the boys are attracted by the ball. Throughout the entire world, the children of the pavements of Rio and Buenos Aires, the kids of the insalubrious districts of

San Paolo in Naples, or the kids of Liverpool and Moss Side, they all have the same dreams. The dream of living with a ball. One day, perhaps, football will be their job. They are convinced that there is nothing more marvellous than the cheer of the crowd which accompanies a ball into the back of the net. And they are right.

When I see them, when they touch me, when they speak to me quietly, I want these boys from Manchester to go away happy and convinced that they have met a player who is more like them than they think. They love a noble sport, even if our dream is daily more and more threatened by the gravediggers of the football business.

But this dream is also something which concerns all of us.

Chapter Five

··

Deceived

L ate in 1991, while playing for Nîmes, came the final incident that persuaded Cantona he could no longer play club football in France. It was to set off a chain of events that would bring him to Old Trafford within the year.

The match against Saint-Etienne is over. I have been sent off for throwing a ball at the referee. I am fed up. Absolutely fed up.

For this action I was summoned to the headquarters of the French football league, to face you, the disciplinary committee, and I was regretting my angry gesture towards the referee. You replied that several clubs had already complained about me. Your justice is then unique in the world – judge and jury, you find means of condemning me, not for the ball thrown at the referee but for other things which concern me that I did a long time ago and for which I have already paid. You then suspended me for a period of four matches, a whole month. You are right. You have not seen me for four years, I understand your gratitude. And when I called each one of you in turn idiots (what a mortal insult!), you have immediately lengthened the suspension by an extra month.

'I ask you only to judge me like any other player in the French league,' I commented to the disciplinary commission some days after I had been sent off in that match.

I have not forgotten the reply of Jacques Riolaci, the president of that commission: 'You can't be judged like any other player. Behind you there is a trail of the smell of sulphur. You can expect anything from an individualist like you.'

Tapie had already promised me the clinic and the straitjacket and here was Riolaci making me seem like a pyromaniac. I knew that it was time for me to leave France and to try to rediscover some tranquillity. Because of all this, I decided that it was time to hang up my boots.

As I write this now, living in England, I am able to breathe again. A little later and I will thank from the bottom of my heart all those who enabled me to take such a decision.

'Living in England, I am able to breathe again.' (A. de Martignac/Presse-Sports)

For a week after my announcement the telephone didn't stop ringing. I didn't lift it up as I did not want to talk to anyone. It's a strange thing to put a full stop to ten years of professionalism, ten years of playing, of pleasure in the stadiums of the whole world, at club level and with the international team, and for some reason or other I had never felt so much at ease.

But one morning I realised that the majority of people get attached to you only out of self-interest. I even had to reassure one of the contractors who was building my house in the Nîmoise countryside that I had sufficient money to pay him. After I decided to stop playing football, he became anxious and was clearly under the impression that I would not be able to honour the building debts. You see, football fame doesn't last a long time, but I was able to reassure him about this. Afterwards, Isabelle and I had a good laugh about this matter. But, from then on, I knew that the celebrity of a player, or what he represents, is only transitory. And whatever happens in the future, this will serve me as a good lesson.

I have voluntarily deprived myself of a game and it is now a fortnight since I stopped playing. How can I live without football? How can I bring up my

70

family? These questions keep coming back to me. I promised Michel Mézy and Jean Bousquet, the directors of Nîmes Olympique, that I would buy my contract. I don't want to owe a centime to the club.

I have no regrets. I am leaving but saying to myself that, with my pal and striking partner Simba and the international team, we could have had a fine time together on the last occasion at the Parc des Princes against Iceland a month ago. So much for the young supporters, whom I promised to score three goals for. I wish that I had never had to leave the world of children.

For nearly a month now I have been present at my own funeral. It's bizarre to be present at your own death. Everyone has come along and said something or other, a lot of it has touched me because I know the people saying it were sincere and they were people whom I admire and people who also know the game.

But, strangely, this hasn't made me change my mind. What have I done since my (provisional) retirement? I have been listening to the singer William Sheller; I have been walking along the beach at Grau-du-Roi; I have been drawing, watching my son grow up, and making plans.

Looking back on that period now, I would say that I was going round in circles then because something was missing, even though I did not wish to admit it. My body and head were in effect so completely accustomed to that physical exercise which comes from training and football effort. I was deprived of that motivation and that thirst which makes you surpass yourself. I was deprived of the need to work and of that energy which you take with you to the stadium. I missed everything: the smells and the ambience of the dressing room, the feeling of belonging to a group, of winning together. I had need for air, for space…and I needed the ball.

Around me everyone was conscious of this lack of something, but no conversation, no requests, no outburst of anger managed to turn me from my desire to stop playing.

And then Michel Platini came to speak to me. Simply. He understood everything. Everything. He knew that I was bursting with the desire to start playing again, but not in this business of old, not in the same conditions which I had had to endure. He knew that I had to get away. He had the impression that I needed to start something new, I had to give myself a new challenge.

We decided to have a look towards England to see if there was an opportunity there.

Why this country?

First of all, there was the practical aspect that the transfer period had not yet ended. Second, however, was the fact that it would be a very dramatic change for me: it would be another culture, another kind of football, another infatuation. In brief, I could restart everything, redo everything, rediscover everything.

And that is how my lawyer, Jean-Jacques Bertrand, and the vice-president of the Syndicate of Professional Footballers of France, Jean-Jacques Amorfini, accompanied by Michel Platini decided to set out on the English trail on my behalf. Within a few weeks I would set out for England.

Later, when I am old, my son Raphaël will say to himself, perhaps when he's looking at me: 'Tell me, then, you didn't waste your time. You had a good life, amusing and very fulfilled. You had the best trade in the world. You could be free. You earned a lot of money. Sometimes you used your name to say some serious things and at other times some lighthearted things. As a footballer you scored many goals. You travelled, you travelled a lot. You had a lot of clubs, a lot of countries – Marseille, Montpellier, Manchester, England and elsewhere. This happened because you had the thirst to be acquainted with everything, to know everything, to love everything. You were in a hurry. We had a good time together. But then above all we know a secret: at the stadium, in a dressing room – whether at Marseille or Manchester or Bordeaux or Leeds or Nîmes – you have always been yourself.'

For the fact that I know these things to be true, how could I ever forget the hand of friendship extended to me by Michel Platini?

Cantona with his great friend Michel Platini. It was Platini who advised him to make the trip to England.
(Presse-Sports)

Everything went very quickly.

The French team manager and his influence had a great effect on my prospects.

Gérard Houllier, who knows England's football just as well as he knows the English language, was entrusted with the task of making the first contacts. He got in touch with Dennis Roach, an agent who has good connections in Great Britain with all the big clubs, and the machine started to roll.

Michel Mézy of Nîmes could no longer keep up with what was going on.

'It's madness. You are starting to wear me out. A month ago you told me that your career is finished and today you are telling me that you want to start playing again in England. I am absolutely worn out, Eric. Empty.'

How could I explain to him this change in my situation? He had done everything in his power to try to persuade me to continue and I had refused to do so. Yet now I was changing my mind.

On 16 December 1991 I had signed the cancellation of my contract with Nîmes Olympique at a moment when I was tired and worn out by all the intrigue which was going on behind the scenes. When I signed this letter I thought I was going to take in a breath of fresh air. But I was wrong.

Undoubtedly, Nîmes Olympique had the impression that they were being swindled in this business. I had been signed up to captain the side, and now I was going. However, it was far from my intention to make them look stupid. My only worry was being able to leave France and for the club to recover the money that it had spent on me. At Nîmes I hadn't been able to express myself on the field; I hadn't been able to obtain the level of play of which I was capable.

There were many reasons for this. One of the most important, it seemed to me, was that I had just had to go through a very difficult period at Marseille, as you will see later. Both Michel Mézy and I were of the opinion that our friendship and confidence, combined with the recent promotion to the first division and the new ambience at the club, would allow me and allow us to live through a real adventure together. But all these marvellous feelings count for nothing when things aren't going well on the pitch.

It is true that we had won a number of games, a dozen I think, but without any panache. We had stolen the matches and I had the feeling that we were putting a lot of effort into things for very little return and the game wasn't giving me any pleasure and the spectacle that we were providing for the spectators wasn't very convincing.

However, I did try very hard to be a good captain. I felt proud to be offered the position and I took the job seriously. I racked my brains to try to find the solutions to our problems, but we were sinking. The public was moaning, they were getting at me, the international who should have been able to or could have been able to transform things. I was being told off for being good when I played for the international team and mediocre when I played for the club.

I was leaving Nîmes at the worst possible moment.

But before going on, I shall tell you how I managed to end up at Nîmes in the first place.

After our victory in the final of the French Cup with Montpellier, Tapie had called me back to Marseille.

I didn't want to go back there. But my contacts with other clubs couldn't lead to any new openings. I belonged to Marseille and they alone could decide my future. I had just had a very good season. Among my achievements were the French Cup, nine goals for the national team, including victories like the one against Germany at Montpellier in February 1990 and that annoyed everybody in Marseille. They wanted me back in their fold.

It was no longer a question of them wanting to loan me or trying to sell me. But I didn't give myself any false illusions. I was going back to Marseille because they had suddenly fallen in love with me (I hadn't changed myself in 18 months) and because they had been forced to appreciate me and to recognise those certain qualities which I have on the field.

The season started well for Marseille: in 12 matches I had scored seven goals. The same was true for the international team as we beat Iceland 2-1 in Reykjavik on 5 September 1990, thanks to goals by Papin and Cantona. Our first hurdle on the way to the European Championships had been cleared. We could look forward to 1992. I was convinced at last that the public in Marseille would love me for my play and nothing else. The jersey that I had thrown down at Sedan was long in the past. And, manifestly, Bernard Tapie no longer had any wish to lock me up in a clinic.

My dream came to an end as early as 28 October 1990 at Marseille against Brest. One of the defenders from the Breton club, Kane, tackled me dangerously from behind near the end of the first half. My knee was damaged: the ligaments were detached and I was out of the game for three months. I worked like a madman to reach my full fitness. I suffered a lot, physically, and my morale sank. Sometimes such an injury can break the career of a footballer. Some weeks after me, for example, Bernard Pardo had the same kind of knock in training and Bernard never played again. So I was lucky.

But another test, worse than that accident, was waiting for me during the period of my recuperation. Franz Beckenbauer, our manager, was giving up the job. A Belgian trainer, Raymond Goethals, was coming to replace him.

I had gained great satisfaction from working with this talented German manager who, just before signing for Marseille, had been crowned world champion in Italy as manager of the victorious German side. Beckenbauer had tried to bring to Marseille a serious professionalism and a code of discipline which, added to his fabulous career as a player, gave me great pleasure. But that wasn't the case for everybody.

The German correctness clashed with the dilettante southern temperament. With him there were no longer any passes to the dressing room, and all the group of crony journalists, mates and friends of friends who gravitated around the team were henceforth told to wait outside the dressing rooms. This small group of locals was annoyed and frustrated at being separated from the players and they caused trouble.

In my opinion, Beckenbauer should have asked himself what sort of club he'd come to, not to mention the worrying fact that he would have to listen to the advice that the president would always wish to give about how the team should be playing. But after Christmas 1990, Beckenbauer decided to hand over the reins to a replacement who was far more malleable and who would not hurt anybody's feelings.

Instead of the class and competence of Beckenbauer, we now had the very individualistic Belgian humour of Raymond Goethals. I am sorry, but the gulf between us was insurmountable. Whereas I had confidence in Beckenbauer as long as he was in the active role as manager, I was now in the era of his successor and it was clear to me that I was going to be given the push. And the reason was quite simple: it had nothing to do with the physical problem linked with my recuperation from injury because I had completely recovered my fitness. I simply did not want to be cast in the mould which had been designed by his majesty Bernard Tapie. It was impossible for me to say that I was playing for the best club in France directed by the most wonderful president on earth and to thank heaven for having sent me there! Nor was there any question of me threatening to go on strike with my team-mates to support the president, Bernard Tapie, who had difficulties with the league for certain insulting comments he had made about a referee. His comments were his own responsibility, not mine.

I found myself given the elbow for not being willing to butter up the president, and I practically didn't play right up to the end of the 1990–91 season.

The Belgian manager Goethals could boast to the press for having taken the decision to get rid of me from the team, but I knew quite well who was pulling his strings. If, on the other hand, he had been told to try to keep me, he would certainly have given me his blessing.

Whatever the case, I wasn't the only one to fall foul of the president of Olympique Marseille: Jean Tigana, Stojkovic, Vercruysse were also placed in the same boat, but perhaps for different reasons.

And that is how the rebellious, undesirable Cantona found himself in Nîmes after an incredible season.

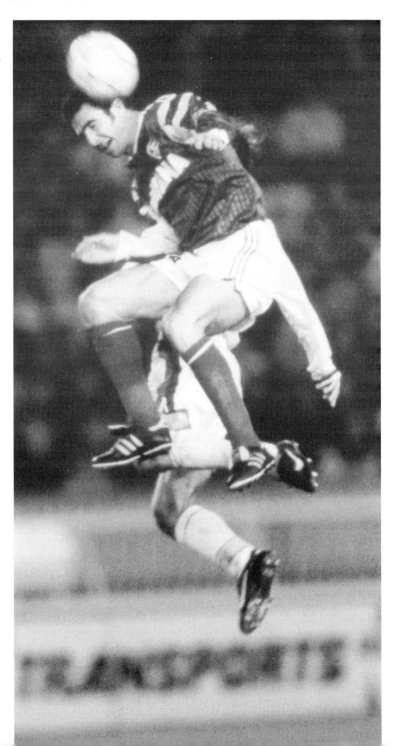

A header for Nîmes, but Cantona was no longer happy in his game.
(Presse-Sports)

In England, Trevor Francis, one of the acquaintances of Michel Platini, had heard about a French player who wanted to leave his home country.

Contacts were quickly established between Jean-Jacques Bertrand and Jean-Jacques Amorfini and Sheffield Wednesday, where Francis had arrived as manager in June 1991. The principal difficulty resided in the fact that I had begun moves to buy out my contract with Nîmes and that I had promised to pay the club damages and interest linked with my transfer. If Sheffield Wednesday wanted me, the British club had to pay ten million francs (about £1 million), the exact sum which Nîmes had paid to Olympique Marseille for my transfer. Sheffield Wednesday did not find this set-up ideal.

On Thursday 23 January 1992, my transfer was being negotiated in Paris in the office of the Mayor of Nîmes, Jean Bousquet. Graham Mackrell, club secretary of Sheffield, was accompanied by the agent Dennis Roach. As Wednesday could not buy me, Nîmes were in a position on the other hand to loan me. After several hours of negotiations, the directors of Nîmes agreed to loan me in some way or another to Sheffield Wednesday.

The meeting had taken place with the greatest of clarity. Graham Mackrell and Dennis Roach had clearly indicated to me that a simple medical was required before the contract was signed with Sheffield Wednesday. There was no mention of any trial period and, anyhow, even if they had proposed such a trial period, I would not have hesitated in telling them that I had not been on trial anywhere since the age of 14, just before I joined Auxerre. The decision was that I would go to Sheffield that Sunday to take part in my first training session and then have the medical.

Everyone knows that the loan between Sheffield Wednesday and Nîmes was not formalised and that I was to make only a very brief stay in Sheffield because there was suddenly a strange story about a prolonged trial period. However, there was also an additional complication to do with money – of commission more precisely. Dennis Roach, who had been approached by Gérard Houllier in order that we should know the names of the clubs which might be interested in me, had at first dealt with clubs who usually pay the agents a commission for realising the transactions with the players. It was obvious that if I had signed a contract for Sheffield he would have got his money. However, he hadn't mentioned a word to me about any trial period. As an established international, this was not something I expected to undertake. On the other hand, for Francis, the manager, this trial period was important as it would give him a chance to get to know me, to judge me. From his point of view, this was fair enough – especially given the added complication that I was an overseas player.

In brief, Francis did not understand why I was refusing to undergo this formality and, for my part, I didn't understand why he was asking for a trial period when I was expecting only a medical visit. This wasn't, however, a problem of language. In the Parisian offices of Jean Bousquet, I, we, everybody, understood what was going on.

In France, they learned very quickly that the bridges between Sheffield Wednesday and myself had been broken. Confusion reigned and, for the media, obviously I once again became the scandalous, unreliable player, the madman.

With the passing of time, this business has made me think again of my puppet in the French version of *Spitting Image*, *Guignols de l'Info*. Most of my friends tell me that the image of 'Picasso', as he is called, is positive, because it makes them laugh and he's not so terrible. They may be right, but I find it to be something extraordinary, stretching credulity to the limit. But what I find strange is the new and distorted picture it can give of someone in public life. 'Picasso' can leave the stage exasperated and use words like 'whore' and 'fuck' and insist that 'PPD', alias Patrick Poivre d'Arvorlui, the eminent TV presenter, says good-day to him. 'Picasso' can paint a red card and show it to himself, and even imagine that he belongs to some imaginary team of birds or animals. In short, on this show, a gesture or word previously considered reprehensible or unreal suddenly becomes funny, comical, and in some strange fashion accepted by public opinion as how I really am. Some see me as my caricature rather than looking at what I do in real life.

Dennis Roach, to redeem himself from this inextricable situation and from all these misunderstandings, reappeared again, this time with Leeds United in his bag.

For several weeks Howard Wilkinson, manager of Leeds, had been trying to get hold of me. But Leeds United make it a policy not to pay commission to the agents and Roach hadn't said anything about their interest. When learning in the evening papers that I was no longer being considered by Sheffield Wednesday, Wilkinson rushed to the telephone: he wanted to see me.

My life story was about to take a new turn.

Chapter Six

···

Honeymoon at Leeds

*A*lthough he was to play only 15 games for Leeds in the run-in to the 1991–2 season, completing a full 90 minutes just five times, Cantona's impact on the club and the fans was immediate. After the problems he had had in France, he was once again doing what he does best.

My career in England began with a kind of Vaudeville which took place in surroundings of old-fashioned decor in a well-to-do hotel.

In Sheffield, the rumour had already spread to the editorial rooms of the *Sun* in London and of the *Yorkshire Evening News* that I had signed for Leeds, but in fact nothing had been formalised following the first contacts with Leeds United.

Dennis Roach and Howard Wilkinson, the manager of Leeds, were to meet us in my room at the end of the afternoon of 31 January 1992. My lawyer, Jean-Jacques Bertrand, would also be present at this meeting. In less than an hour of conversation, the most important things had been said. Wilkinson wanted me. He had been persuaded that he needed to sign me because of the absence through injury of his striker Lee Chapman, and Leeds wanted to give some muscle to its attack and the manager of Leeds was ready to put his confidence in me.

At that time Leeds United and their greatest rivals Manchester United were well ahead in the title race. The two clubs were already nine points ahead of Liverpool in third place. The Championship of England would be decided between these two fraternal enemies from the north of England.

Certainly, Wilkinson hadn't wasted any time or opportunity to find out from Michel Platini and Gérard Houllier about my way of playing. Houllier was the French coach perhaps best versed in the ways of English football, having studied at Liverpool University. While there he had been a regular visitor to Anfield and had maintained his English contacts since then. But this was merely a sensible step for Wilkinson before taking such a big decision. Besides that, the manager made light of my tumultuous past and the reputation it had brought me. The passion of Elland Road would satisfy all my ambitions, he was sure.

It was strange, here was I looking for the calm and tranquillity that had been lost in my everyday life in France and nevertheless I was already becoming conscious of the popular delirium which football inspires in Great Britain.

Football has always unleashed great passions here. Tattoos on the arm, tears spilt when a star player leaves – emotion is everywhere. In the stands of Old Trafford, thousands of fathers have called their sons George in memory of one of the greatest football stars in the history of Manchester United: Northern Ireland's George Best. It's the same thing in the Kop of Liverpool. During those mad Keegan years between 1971 and 1977, hundreds of small Kevins were born in the city of the Beatles and it must be said that Kevin Keegan is now a part of the legend of Liverpool.

In saying yes to Howard Wilkinson, I did not quite appreciate the pressure that was waiting for me. My new manager invited me the next day to watch the match between Leeds United and Notts County. Our conversation lasted a little more than an hour. Certainly no contract had yet been signed, but we knew quite well that a mutual adventure would soon be bringing us together. There would be no question of a trial period. My examination would take place on the field. Perhaps even in the next match at Oldham, if I felt that I was ready.

The new chant at Elland Road: 'Ooh, aah, Cantona!'
(Empics)

Howard Wilkinson gets his message across during a training session with Leeds United. (Colorsport)

I would like Howard Wilkinson to know, and the public of Elland Road with him, that Leeds had given me back my life. I came back to football thanks to him and that incomparable welcome which was given to me when I arrived at Leeds. Together we would prepare to become champions of England. It would not be long before the fans at Elland Road would be singing as a choir 'Ooh, aah, Cantona!', the chant that became so popular after our victories. The evening of my greatest goal in the colours of Leeds United against Chelsea on 11 April, Wilkinson would realise that I had done something so spectacular that it would be remembered by all British fans for a long time. And, after that, it's not important to talk about the ruptures and arguments which would surface later.

In his heart, Wilkinson knew quite well that I had also helped to revitalise Leeds United at a crucial period of the season. From Oldham to Chelsea and from Liverpool to Luton my heart beats to the rhythm of the fans. I have forgotten nothing about Leeds. I have forgotten nothing about you, the supporters, who came in thousands to acclaim the team after we had won the title. I will never forget your applause or your generosity, which I found so dazzling. You would have to be a great cynic not to remember the great and simple happiness which ran in the veins of the Leeds United fans the evening when they celebrated our title of champions of England.

The shape of my life shows that I am always on the move, whatever the club is, whatever the town is that welcomes me. I have suffered too much from becoming attached to things. In Marseille, three months after a knee injury, I understood that the hours of work I had put in and the pain I had suffered in order to recover my best form were of no interest to others. I was mad. I would have done anything to bathe again in the lights of the Vélodrome of Marseille, but however, after some training sessions, a celebrated trainer walked in front of me, his head lowered, not wishing to see me.

Howard Wilkinson had been very clear with me from the first training sessions: he was convinced that I could rapidly impose myself on Leeds United, but he also let me understand that he didn't want to push me too quickly. English clubs, it is true, display a certain distrust of foreign players. Their football is made out of aerial duels, of hard running and of tackles which cannot be endured unless a player's physical condition is almost perfect. The British establishment also thinks that while a footballer who comes from the south of Europe may have irreproachable technical skills they do not believe that his body will be able to stand up to the strains of the northern football. And here again, with the advantage of the time that has passed, I can better appreciate the judgement and opinions of Michel Platini and Gérard Houllier, who helped me to cross the Channel. They knew quite well that my heart and my legs were made to get on with British football.

It was on 8 February 1992 that I made my first acquaintance with league football in England. I came on in the second half against Oldham, but we lost 2-0.

Then, on 29 February, on a Saturday afternoon at Elland Road, a great joy came to the Cantona family. Leeds United were playing Luton Town. Howard Wilkinson sent me on after 20 minutes following an injury to Tony Dorigo. As soon as I came on I knew I felt good and that I was going to score my first goal in the colours of Leeds United before the fans massed in the stands of Elland Road. There is nothing more paradoxical nor more breathtaking than a goal in front of a crowd which is waiting for it. At that exact moment when the ball went into the net, thousands of supporters behind the goal seemed to plunge towards the turf.

This is an image which only British football is capable of giving. Here it's like a cry which rattles a cathedral. Whether you are having a good or a bad match, the public will sing profound and grave songs and then, at a stroke, as the ball hits the back of the net, thousands of voices sing at the same instant with their arms outstretched. It's pure ecstasy.

In scoring this goal at the Kop end I became seduced. I had met, it seemed, my new family.

Cantona makes his debut for Leeds against Oldham, 8 February 1992. (Colorsport)

Certainly, there were to be other emotions, other great spectacles but the victory over Luton brought me the new joy of scoring a goal for Leeds. That evening Raphaël, in Nîmes with Isabelle, saw his papa score a goal in England for the first time.

The club management had rented a house for me in the countryside near Leeds. We continued to live there for a long while after my arrival. The house and the district are definitely not plush or exclusive, making the atmosphere very pleasing to me. Many of our neighbours were Pakistanis or West Indians, as well as English. They were straightforward, friendly and generous. I preferred by far our little English house with its wild piece of garden to those vast Victorian houses among which I am sure I would soon get fed up. Even when I was playing for Manchester United, I loved to leave the hotel in Manchester where I stayed during the week to go back to my house. Often, I arranged to meet Raphaël when he came out of school and both of us went and played football in the grounds of Roundhay Park, which was situated quite close to our house. We had a good time there.

As for me, using the language of the Spanish bullfight, I stuck a fine *banderille* in the neck of Luton. But the most important thing was to build on that. Gradually I was winning the confidence of Wilkinson and the other players at Elland Road were becoming accustomed to my kind of play. The day would soon arrive for one of my most inspired moments, an incident that would remain engraved in the memory of the Leeds supporters.

This day came at Elland Road on 11 April 1992. We were playing against Chelsea. It is difficult to describe the out-of-the-ordinary goal that I scored on that day. In three touches I deceived the defenders who were coming to tackle me, without the ball touching the ground and then finally placed the ball in the far corner of the net. About ten minutes remained and throughout the whole of that time the fans stood up in the stands, singing and chanting. It was a very moving and extraordinary experience.

I believe that that is also the tremendous insolence of youth. You have to think that anything is possible, whatever the difficulties, and it is inevitable there will be some, that will confront you. Why do they show such enthusiasm? Not because of your appearance or because such-and-such a player is more of a media person than another. I believe, rather, that the public wishes to thank anyone who is trying to make him dream.

Today football has almost lost that chance for a gratuitous piece of football skill because there are too many financial interests present in the game. Even though the fans love it, players will not risk juggling with the ball in the middle of a match in case it costs the club dearly. Such skills can only be displayed when there is no money at stake. The moment suffices to itself. It is marvellous when it comes off. It is wearying when it fails. But it never leaves you indifferent. And it was that evening that I heard the first 'Ooh, aah, Cantona!' chants which were going to accompany me wherever I went, from Elland Road and later to Old Trafford.

The end of the season with Leeds was full of passion. Right to the very end we were neck and neck with Manchester United. All around the club the possibility of winning the title unleashed passions. Leeds, champions of

England in 1969 and 1974, finalists in the Champions' Cup in 1975, were beginning to dream again. The glory days of their famous manager, Don Revie, had returned.

This title, my first in England, wasn't going to escape us. And it was in an atmosphere of warm celebration and pride, especially when you stop to consider the rivalry that exists between Leeds and Manchester, that we were going to mark this coronation.

The directors of Leeds had organised a tour of the city centre. It would be a happy occasion. After 26 April, when the title was secured, I and the other players slept very little because we were all so excited. Everywhere, the city was draped in the colours of the club – on balconies and in windows. Even faces were painted blue and white. Thousands of fans celebrated the occasion.

On the balcony of the town hall, all the team assembled and we were given a great ovation. They sang and it was even sunny. I took the microphone which they gave me so that I could say a few words to all the people, as

Leeds celebrate becoming league champions in 1992. (Colorsport)

tradition requires, and I said to the supporters: 'Why I love you, I don't know why, but I love you.'

This phrase eventually became the title of a record which was made by two musicians who were supporters of Leeds. Leeds will always have a place in my heart, because it is there that I recaptured my taste for football and where the supporters welcomed me in a way which has rarely happened to me.

The European Championships in Sweden in 1992 were once again a time of disappointment for Cantona, despite the side's perfect record during qualification. The pattern was to be repeated in the attempt to get to the States in 1994, when early form deserted the French.

After all these emotions in winning the title, there was no question of rest. I had to go straight to France to prepare for another challenge, this time with the national team: the European Championship finals of 1992, held in the middle of June in Sweden.

We were very confident. To gain qualification for this final phase we had played eight matches – and won all eight. We had been first in our group and such was our domination in the qualifying rounds that we were made many people's favourites for the European title.

Unfortunately, it was a great anti-climax. Only a few words come to my mind to talk about the disappointment which awaited us: favourite, inexperience, sadness. Our elimination wasn't, however, an injustice but I am unable to give you other reasons. There isn't any reason. Or perhaps there are a thousand reasons. But it's too late and I've already brooded too much about it.

Since then, however, we have overcome this disappointment and after the first year of qualifying games we were well placed to participate in the World Cup in the United States in 1994 after

France beat Finland 2-1 in Paris on 14 November 1992, just one of their victories in a successful start to their World Cup campaign. (Guizbaud/Sport+)

◀ *Cantona lifts the championship trophy and savours his first title in England.* (Colorsport)

our victories over Austria (twice), Finland, Israel and Sweden, and only one defeat – against Bulgaria. That was a great comeback after what happened in Sweden and perhaps the experience helped us to be reborn. Certainly things went well for me in those games, because I scored five of our goals.

But many things have happened since Sweden. A new team manager, Gérard Houllier, and new players have arrived in the international team, as if to rub out the past and help us to revive our winning ways.

Michel Platini went soon after the European Championships. And this departure didn't please me. I was very disappointed in our failure in Sweden and sorry to lose the person for whom I would even have played in goal if he had asked me. Platini is the one for whom I had and have and will always have an eternal respect and admiration.

It took me some time to get over the sadness which followed our last match defeat against Denmark, a happy and unexpected team which was to go on to take the title, and also to get over the disappointment of Platini's departure, to whom I owe so much. I would have wished, and we all would have wished, so loved was he, that he had left with the victory which his stature and talent merited.

It was in this state of mind that I set off as quickly as possible to holiday alone at my parents' house in the Alps in order to breathe the fresh air and distance myself from a season which had been extremely tense and draining, with peaks of joy and happiness and depths of pain, just like the chain of mountains in the Alps, with all its contrasts, where I was going to rest and paint.

One of the aspects of Cantona's character that marks him out from most other footballers is his love of the arts. Few, if any, footballers currently playing in the Premiership would have heard of De Staël or Ambrogiani, let alone be able to write as eloquently about them as he did in his autobiography:

I have always loved painting. Quite simply because my father drew me towards it.

I was eight when I first discovered all the shades and colours of the universe in his workshop, which my father had built in an attic underneath the rafters. It was the other play room of my childhood. In the daytime there was school and football. In the evening there was the workshop. I have never sought to understand why I was attracted to such a place when my two brothers turned away from it. In addition, my father had not received any individual training in art from his family, but I knew that it wasn't just an apprenticeship in painting that I had received. It was also another way of looking at the world.

I am not the first to have said that every artistic activity tends, in one fashion or another, to embellish the world in which we live. When you become attached to beauty at an early age, it's very difficult to renounce it. A good footballer is by nature a beautiful footballer and I already knew that perfection in this area was a paradise very difficult to reach. In the history of our game, only a few players have had the happiness to reach it: Pelé, Maradona, Platini and Cruyff.

Bowled over by the playing of colours, the speed at which the light changed, the contrasts, De Staël confessed in a letter his inability to commit to canvas so much beauty. Some may be astonished that a professional footballer can see his trade as being like a work of art. But I have found in the painting of Nicolas De Staël that his commentaries comprise a response to all those who try to be funny and make a joke about a footballer's perception of his own craft.

In truth, there is no finer childhood than that which is divided between sport and the imaginary. My father would often take me to the galleries to discover the latest works of Ferrari or Pierre Ambrogiani. He opened my eyes to the 'Fauves' – Camoin or Auguste Chabaud. With time, the love I held for the Marseillais school of painting has grown.

I thank my father for very early on in my life giving me the opportunity to familiarise myself with the world of Ambrogiani. It seems to me that his art has been able to go even further than the Impressionists' movement was able to manage. Looking at the pictures of Ambrogiani, I see the beauty of those vivid and sometimes violent colours of Provence and its sky. The essential lines of the art explode in this type of painting.

I remember when I was only 15 and I had just arrived at Auxerre. One of my favourite players was decked out with a name worthy of the Italian Renaissance: Giancarlo Antognoni. He played in the centre of midfield in the World Cup-winning Italian squad in 1982. He did not manage to achieve a great career, but that's of little importance. Between the '70s and 1984 he lit a candle in the Italian league. He was nicknamed 'the archangel with feet of velvet'. I remember only that he was capable of turning a match without doing the slightest harm to his adversary. His touch on the ball was unique.

It is necessary for those in charge of football to understand that there is no salvation without the artist. Quite rightly you have to win, but you've also got to be able to admit defeat so that football can keep its source of emotion. It is also true that, in defeat, curious as it may seem, it is always the artists who can drink to victory or defeat.

I like the words of Jacques Thibert, I believe, when he wrote the following about Maradona, Anquetil and other geniuses from the world of sport: 'Here are the high-wire artists of the soul, people who can do the impossible, who are on another plane. They are flawless only in the expression of their sporting excellence.'

An artist, in my eyes, is someone who can lighten up a dark room. I have never and will never find any difference between the pass from Pelé to Carlos Alberto in the final of the World Cup in 1970 in Mexico and the poetry of the young Rimbaud, who stretches 'cords from steeple to steeple and garlands from window to window'. There is in each of these human manifestations an expression of beauty which touches us and gives us a feeling of eternity.

Look at the final of the 100 metres in the World Championships in Tokyo in the summer of 1991: Carl Lewis got off to a bad start, failing to get out of his starting blocks quickly. His body only wakes up about 40 metres into the race. Fifty metres from the finishing line, Lewis is a beaten man. But an acceleration came from the depths of the night and propelled him towards victory and a new world record. The pictures of this race will get old. The photographs will go yellow. But the memory of sport will never forget that race. Lewis, that day, was an artist touched by grace.

It was in Martigues in the month of April 1986 that I learned of the death of Pierre Ambrogiani. A part of my dreams had suddenly disappeared. Ambrogiani was an old man of over 80, but I found it difficult to accept his death. Life is such that this kind of news often comes to us during a joyful morning. Ambrogiani took away with him my wanderings in the streets of Marseille and my strolls among men in the art galleries. A page of my childhood was turned.

Chapter Seven

···

The Legend of
Manchester United

*W*hat had started so well for Cantona at Leeds suddenly turned sour, and Howard Wilkinson sold him to Alex Ferguson at Manchester United for £1.2 million. It was to be the bargain of the decade, but there were those who said it was Ferguson's biggest risk, citing Cantona's wanderlust, which made Old Trafford his eighth home in as many years, and his disciplinary record. Here Cantona explains what went wrong at Leeds and his delight at joining the biggest and most famous club in England. If the critics had their doubts, Cantona, Ferguson and the United fans did not.

It's 6 February 1958 and the plane bringing back the players, directors and supporters of Manchester United is having difficulty with take-off. On the runway at Munich airport the BEA Elizabethan is attempting to take off for the third time. Two attempts have already been made, but the weight of the snow and the ice on the plane have stopped it from flying off. It's growing dark, it's snowing, it's windy. Inside the plane is the best and most ambitious team in world football, the creation of Matt Busby, commander-in-chief of the Manchester United troops. The third take-off is also the last and it will finish with 23 people dead, including some of the most gifted footballers of their generation…

Here at Old Trafford, everyone remembers this with great emotion. The directors of the club told me about it as soon as I arrived at the club. But I already knew. The city will never forget it.

From the ruins of the plane which crashed that night at the end of the runway at Munich, the bodies of captain Roger Byrne, Geoff Bent, Bill Whelan, Eddie Colman, Tommy Taylor, Mark Jones, David Pegg and Duncan Edwards are brought out. The previous night the team had played Red Star Belgrade and had drawn 3-3 to set up a place in the European Cup semi-final. Now they were plunged into the darkest night in the history of United. For a

Cantona made his first Wembley appearance for an English club in the 1992 Charity Shield, scoring a hat-trick to help Leeds to victory over Liverpool. Rod Wallace joins in the celebration. (Colorsport)

'8 August 1992 was one of the best days in my career.' (Colorsport)

while, Matt Busby's life also hung in the balance.

I have been told all about this in Manchester and also in Leeds. I know also that the club, still managed by Matt Busby, had begun to live again one evening on 29 May 1968. On that day, United beat Benfica of Lisbon 4-1 in the final at Wembley and gave England its first European crown. The captain of the Red Devils was none other than Bobby Charlton, survivor of the Munich disaster. Manchester had destroyed Benfica, inspired by the genius of Eusebio, thanks, among other things, to the two *enfants terribles*: George Best of Northern Ireland and Brian Kidd. Wembley would give any of its springs in exchange for that spring of 29 May 1968.

Let's speak of legends. I had just left Leeds United, champions of England for the third time in its history, and was getting ready to join the most famous club in the world. Along with Juventus of Turin, Manchester United has the greatest number of supporters throughout the world. During my first days in Manchester, I was astonished to receive mail from Singapore, Tokyo, Ankara and New York. But I soon got used to the huge interest in the club.

Normally, a professional footballer, even one who is fond of travelling and discoveries, takes only a very superficial interest in the history of a club, even if it is his own. But here in England it's different. History is everywhere. There are museums in the stadiums of all the famous clubs. You can see there, among the trophies, old photographs and the kit which the players used to wear, the history of all those who took part at one time or another in the great adventure. It is all very moving and above all it's proof that the past glories of a club aren't forgotten and that an effort is made to remember all those who have contributed in one way or another to the building or enhancing of the honours of a club.

How did I come to find myself at Manchester United, the legendary club with a past so glorious and so painful?

After the European Championship in Sweden in June 1992 and the departure of Platini as France's manager, I started training with Leeds in preparation for the new season. Our first big game was to be against Liverpool, the FA Cup winners, in the Charity Shield at Wembley.

To play at Wembley, for a footballer, in terms of the prestige and honour which emanate from playing there, is a little like Wimbledon for a tennis player, with the guarantee that you will be watched by over 70,000 spectators as you play on the most wonderful surface in the world.

I will never forget it. I even think that 8 August 1992, when I succeeded in scoring three goals in the temple of football, was one of the best days in my career. The national anthem, the chants and shouts of the supporters, the stadium full of the colours of both teams playing against each other, the presentation of the trophy – I remember everything.

After that match, the Championship began at a pace which is typical of English football. That is to say, completely hectic. In all, 22 clubs take part in the Premier League, on average two to four more than in the other European leagues, and with two cups to play for, plus, for some, the European competitions – this means that for most of the time top clubs like Manchester United are playing twice a week throughout the season without any winter break. It's a very saturated fixture list, especially if you compare it with France, where there are only 20 clubs and one cup to play for, as well as a short break around Christmas. In addition, practically the whole of the United squad are international players, and games for their respective countries merely add to the pressure.

Leeds got off to a moderate start in the league, but we were able to rekindle

Leeds finally overcame Stuttgart in the first round of the European Cup, but were knocked out by Rangers in the next. (Popperfoto)

the flame of our supporters by offering them a match in the European Cup against Stuttgart. We lost the first leg 3-0, and seemed set for an immediate exit from the competition. However, at Elland Road we played some great football, spurred on by our fans, and won 4-1. Because of the away goals rule we would have gone out, despite this sparkling performance. But Stuttgart had fielded too many foreign players so we were forced to meet a third time, in Barcelona. There, thanks to goals from Gordon Strachan and Carl Shutt, we won 2-1.

What followed, unfortunately, was less glorious. We were eliminated from the Coca-Cola Cup by Watford of the First Division, then from the European Cup when we were finally defeated by Glasgow Rangers in what was seen as the championship of Britain. A third of the way through the season and we were in mid-table in the league – a mediocre record for the champions.

For my part, in the 20 matches I played for Leeds that season, all competitions included, I had still managed to score 11 goals.

But there were problems. I began to have increasing difficulty in decoding the language used by my manager. When I say 'decoding' that means understanding what Wilkinson is trying to get at. His comments were strange and rather incoherent, in my opinion. One moment he would tell me that he wants me to know that I owe everything to him, that I am only a Frenchman lost in the English league and at other times he would say to me that without me the team is nothing and that I am the essential part.

I did not understand the use of such contradictory messages. If you look at the figures and the statistics of my contribution to the team, he had no reason to reproach me for anything. He was unable to criticise my attitude to training or my relations with my team-mates. I discussed these problems with my family, but I was at a loss to understand what was going on. What did he want from me? I was adored by the Leeds fans, I was working as hard as ever. But nevertheless our relationship continued to get worse. The fact of the language problem did not help matters, either.

'You put him in the shade,' Leeds supporters told me after my departure. I can't believe that this was the reason. However, it became more and more clear that he wanted to get rid of me.

In a short time the fortunes of the club had been transformed. We were languishing in the middle of the league when everybody had been dreaming of a glorious run in the European Cup and of retaining the league title. In such circumstances, perhaps it was felt that Wilkinson did not need the Frenchie any more and the attraction which I represented. Perhaps he thought I was too much of an individual to fit into the sort of team spirit they were relying upon to pull themselves up. But it was clear that it was difficult to make the supporters swallow that pill when, at the announcement of my departure, the switchboard at the club was completely jammed and people came *en masse* to express their disgust and to tear up their season tickets.

Wilkinson tried to explain his decision by peddling the rumour that I did not accept his authority and that he must be the only boss. To justify his version of events, he had to let me go to one of his greatest rivals for a sum which was far lower than my value. This was clear evidence that he was ready at all costs, even financial, to ensure that I left. It was a well-planned move by him. The supporters were confused and did not know who they should believe.

All the while, Wilkinson continued to repeat his comments to reassure the fans and to justify his position. Suddenly, within two weeks, I had become a traitor to Leeds, so soon after having been a hero.

I know that he forced me to leave. The curious thing is that it was not the only time that he had acted in such a way with players who were well-liked by the supporters. Vinny Jones and John Sheridan had both previously found themselves in the same uncomfortable position. It is clear from all this that he does not like strong personalities who have a rapport with the fans.

Fortunately, at the time when my difficulties with the Leeds United manager were increasing, Alex Ferguson of Manchester United was looking for a striker. When Wilkinson mentioned on the phone that I was available, Ferguson knew that I was the player he needed. In an afternoon the transfer was concluded. I knew that I was joining the sworn enemy of the Leeds fans, but also that it was the most prestigious club in Great Britain, with a team that had been on the verge of greatness for the last couple of years.

My excitement is beyond belief on 27 November 1992, the day after my transfer. Before starting my first training session with Alex Ferguson, my new manager, two images came clearly to my mind.

My father had told me on many occasions how Bobby Charlton scored a goal against the great AC Milan in the semi-final of the European Cup in 1969. Bobby Charlton, winner of the World Cup in 1966, European Cup winner in 1968, is still working for Manchester United. He has come almost to symbolise the club, just like the other heroes of those unforgettable times – George Best, Denis Law, and others. They are real, living legends, better than any ambassadors, who ensure that the prestige and grandeur of Manchester United will continue. These icons from the past come now to Old Trafford to watch us play and they speak to us in the dressing rooms which they have not ceased to haunt. By contrast, French clubs seem to me to be far more capricious and selective in the memories that they hold of the great players who have made a contribution to their clubs.

The other impression that I had of the club I had just joined was far more recent. The players whom I was joining at Manchester had won the Cup-Winners' Cup in 1991, beating Barcelona 2-1. This was no mean exploit, but what was more, it showed that the club was capable of competing with and beating the very best in Europe.

I knew practically everyone in the side by name or by reputation. There was Bryan Robson, of course, the captain; Peter Schmeichel, the goalkeeper who had won the European Championship with Denmark; Gary Pallister, Steve Bruce, Denis Irwin and Paul Parker, who between them formed a solid defence. Brian McClair the Scot, Paul Ince, who had just broken into the England side, Andrei Kanchelskis the Russian were in midfield – and they were all internationals. Then among the young ones there was Lee Sharpe and Ryan Giggs, the Welshman. It was a marvellous cosmopolitan mixture, just like the European Community about which people speak so much. I cannot forget Mark Hughes, another Welshman, who would play centre forward alongside me. Everyone had told me that our temperaments would clash. The reply to that came on the pitch, in the dressing room and on the training field. But the best answer that I can give is the record of our partnership: in the 20 games we started together in the 1992–3 league season United scored 39 goals.

Besides, it is frequently true to say that my personality is different to the attacker alongside whom I play. In the French side, for example, with Jean-Pierre Papin, it is the same thing. It's obvious that he and I are different, but we have learned to get to know each other, to understand each other's strengths. On the field we are able to link up in our play and so we can be certain our partnership and our effectiveness have been proved. The combination of Hughes and Cantona was also to prove itself during the season.

When I came to Manchester in November 1992, the club undoubtedly had the best defence in the league – but not the best attack, scoring just 18 goals in 17 games. United were then sixth in the league and off course for the Championship. Our team was nine points behind the leaders, Norwich City. However, in less than three months, far from drowning, we had begun to cruise. I was not for certain the Messiah, but I was delighted that things went well as it proved to those, like some French journalists, for example, that they would not be able to dance on my dead body. The simple fact is that I liked being in this team and in its ambience.

The brilliant players who surrounded me made it much easier for me to slot into the team. The quick play, usually on the ground, which is rare in England, and the high technical ability, precise and sure, allowed me to develop. It gave me a sight of how British football could be played. We were

Cantona memorabilia has always sold apace in the souvenir shop at Manchester United – it has moved on from shirts to masks. (Empics)

practising the continental style of passing and movement, but without turning our backs on the strengths of the British approach: pressure, determination and solidarity.

I was happy to belong to this great new Manchester United side. The tee-shirts, bobble hats and postcards with my picture began to sell at the souvenir shop at Manchester United and this was a sign that I was becoming accepted as a member of the family.

In those first three months after my arrival, having signed for Manchester United at the end of November, everything had sped by. I made my debut in the new colours on 6 December at Old Trafford against Manchester City, our great derby rivals, replacing the injured Ryan Giggs at half-time.

The proliferation of matches around Christmas and the New Year is deliberate. It enables the public, especially the children on holiday from school, to take advantage of the break to come in great numbers to Old Trafford to celebrate Christmas with us. With regard to presents, I think that that year we spoilt our supporters.

On 19 December I scored my first goal for United at Chelsea, where we drew 1-1 and on the 26th we set off for Sheffield Wednesday. What was more important than the one point we eventually brought back from Sheffield that evening was the manner in which we obtained it. I have no doubt in my own mind that it was this match which marked an important stage in our road towards final victory.

Twenty minutes from the end of the match, before nearly 40,000 spectators at Hillsborough, we were losing 3-0. In an incredible turnabout, we pulled back the score to 3-3 and I had the personal satisfaction and pride of scoring the equalising goal. But it was this reversal of the situation which clearly illustrated our determination never to believe that we were beaten, even when all the evidence seemed to point that way. It was to be one of the keys to our success.

Two days later, on the 28th, we played in front of our own crowd and dominated Coventry City, who had just beaten both Liverpool and Aston

The Manchester derby,
6 December 1992: Cantona
makes his debut for United
at Old Trafford.
(Colorsport)

Cantona has just scored
the equaliser in a dramatic
3-3 draw with Sheffield
Wednesday on Boxing
Day 1992. (Colorsport)

99

Villa, to win 5-0. It was the same scenario on 9 January 1993, when we welcomed Tottenham and there was the same euphoria when we won 4-1 to the cheers and applause of our 36,000 supporters. We were now top of the league and challenged the rest to try to keep up with us.

On 8 February, Manchester United were away again, but this time it was at

Leeds v Manchester United, 8 February 1993: the atmosphere at Elland Road is supercharged for 'the return of the traitor'. To the delight of the hostile Leeds fans Cantona is booked in the 30th minute. (Empics)

Leeds, my former club. The stadium was full and the British press and television stations were delighted at the idea of being present at 'the return of the traitor'. In England, the media publicity and pressure are much more intense than in France, and the newspapers and television had created a tension and pressure around my return to Elland Road throughout the previous week. Perhaps they were hoping for some kind of scene, a fight. They were scrutinising every little thing I did. So it was that I was reproached for spitting as I was leaving the ground. All I did was merely to spit at a wall, but there were those who were keen to suggest that it was something else, that I was showing contempt for the fans who had been cheering me a few months before. Given the collective hysteria that reigned that day at the stadium, the atrocious atmosphere that had been orchestrated for the arrival of Cantona and Manchester United, the incident was quite laughable.

Like all great clubs, Manchester United is at the same time venerated and detested, feared and envied throughout the country. But with Leeds fans there is a quite distinctive and special hostility. Their supporters and the United fans hate each other in a fashion I find difficult to understand. I think that, if I'd not gone to United, the tension surrounding my return to Elland Road would certainly not have taken on such great proportions.

Forty miles separate the two cities. It would be a mere walk for a tourist who wanted to discover the countryside of the north and the Yorkshire Dales. But it's the depth of the night for anyone who goes over to the enemy. In crossing the Pennines, I had become a traitor. The Leeds fans had drawn aeroplanes crashing down with the date of 6 February 1958 written on them (what a sense of humour!) to try to goad the Manchester supporters who, in return, shouted back at them 'thanks very much for selling Eric to us!' The insults rained down, but they were mostly typical of the kind of banal hostile chants you often hear at English stadiums during derby matches between local rivals.

Leeds United was now behind me. I was able to concentrate on Manchester United and the future. But I could not forget those events in the past that had brought me to this position.

Chapter Eight

· ·

The Race for the Championship

anchester United had waited 26 years for the league title. Finally, in 1993, it was to be theirs – thanks largely to the influence of the inspirational Frenchman, who was going for his third successive title, having won at Marseille and Leeds the two previous years. Writing in the immediate aftermath of that time, he recalls the drama and tension of the last couple of months in the 1992–3 season – and the celebrations that followed once the title was secured:

It is 14 March 1993 and Aston Villa have come to the famous stadium of Old Trafford. The leaders against the team in second place, both sides are equal on points. It had been clear to me for some time, especially after losing out to Leeds the previous season, that Manchester United were not going to be satisfied with second place. There had been too many dramas, too many disappointments, accumulated over time for such an outcome to be honourable and sufficient to console the city.

I knew that the youth of Manchester was going to make Old Trafford explode that day.

For 26 years Manchester United had been searching for the league title. Nothing is more terrible for a city in love with football than when victory continues to escape it. The FA Cup in 1990, the Cup-Winners' Cup the following year, the Rumbelows League Cup in 1992 – they were all great triumphs, but insufficient to silence the opponents or sceptics.

The year before, when winning the Championship at Leeds United, I had witnessed the distress of the Reds. They had come so close to great happiness and so this time Alex Ferguson intended to go all the way.

The match is a complete sell-out. Old Trafford is full to bursting point with over 36,000 spectators. Big clubs have a soul which floats from south to north and from east to west in the stadium whenever a vital match is being played. Dignified old ladies who come to the game tell you with great sincerity about the genius of Duncan Edwards, mown down in full flight at the age of 21, the dribbling ability of Best, the marvellous insolence of Brian Kidd, the vision of

14 March 1993: Manchester United take on league leaders Aston Villa at Old Trafford. The match ends in a 1-1 draw and the points remain equal. (Empics)

Bobby Charlton, and all these images that surround and protect the Red Devils.

It was, however, Aston Villa who opened fire.

Something extraordinary happens in the English stands when the home team is being beaten or perhaps dominated. The songs become louder to cheer on the wounded soldiers. It's then that the players and supporters are part of the same family, the same clan. There's no visible separation between the player and the spectator. There is complete harmony of identification. A club of the size and stature of Manchester United could quite easily protect its players when they arrive at the stadium and keep the crowd away from them. They don't do that because the supporters are an integral part of the club. They laugh in victory and cry in defeat.

Old Trafford had been staggered by this cannonball from Steve Staunton of Aston Villa, but we decided not to take it lying down. We knew we had to equalise so that they would not get ahead of us in the league. We had to be at our best in a match which had been billed as a Championship decider, even though both teams had nine more games to play.

In the 67th minute of the match Paul Ince spreads a long ball wide to the left to McClair. His cross is well weighted and, as I jump, I see that Mark Hughes has taken up a good position in the penalty area. A deflection with my head towards the Welshman. It's billiards in the sky at Old Trafford. Mark Hughes heads in front of goal. A goal! United have equalised. Old Trafford is beside itself.

This match was generally considered to be one of the finest seen for a long time at the ground. There were very few technical errors by either side, marvellous pieces of combination, some fine individual play, vivacity. It was 'a lesson in football', as the newspapers described it, given by two teams who were the main contenders for the league title of England, both playing at the summit of their art. After a shower, my exit from a crowded and excited stadium was one of the most difficult I had encountered.

But that's so typical of England. Here, people come to the ground as a family, with wife and children, sometimes as early as midday. The players have their last team talk with the manager before the match at the stadium, in close proximity to the field. This allows us to hear all those who have come to see us play. It is a moving experience to listen to the singing even before we emerge from the tunnel.

This is why I shall never forget meeting a blind supporter in one of the hospitality rooms at Elland Road some months earlier in the season. This fan kept on telling me about his admiration for my play. We had just beaten Everton 2-0 and I went over to where he was sitting. 'I have supported Leeds United for many decades,' he told me. 'I know you without seeing you. But I don't want you to leave me this evening without shaking my hand.'

This handshake was frank and brief. I have discovered that in England the fans do not resemble those of any other country in any way. Here, the fans have a need to touch their idols, to speak to them. The exchange is always very short. In some way, the players are simply brothers sailing in the same boat; a boat called football. They're all fighting for the same cause. The exchange between fans and players is very rapid, but of a proximity which I had not been used to in France.

I know that the population of the industrial north of England has a reputation for independence and originality. In the course of the matches I have played, and in the time that I have spent there, I have got the clear message from the spectators that they appreciated the fact that I was different from the rest. In an environment so full of conformism, I believe that this was very much appreciated by the direct and straightforward English people.

All the same, I cannot forget that towns like Liverpool, Leeds and Manchester have been ravaged by the economic problems in Great Britain. Liverpool now has more people on the dole than footballers on the grass. It's a long time since England ruled an immense colonial empire which enabled it to boast about the riches of the Indies.

Manchester remains, however, one of the great sporting cities of the world and was a candidate for the Olympic Games of the year 2000. But its youth continues to make its sounds of rebellion in the pubs and in the warehouses which have been closed down. I feel very close to this sharp and lively young generation. Perhaps in time attitudes will change, but nobody can deny that here, beneath the windows of the inner city of Manchester, there is an intense love of football, for celebration and music. There is a strong will and desire to live. The parents of these children still recall the exploits of Best, Law and Charlton in the 1960s. And today their children come to support us and to shout for us. These boys and girls of 15, who dance and sing in the big nightclubs in Manchester like the Hacienda, near to the university, are those who are also thrilled to sing for us every Saturday.

It was all very well playing on 14 March in what seemed to me to be a fine game against Aston Villa, but we were far from being league champions. I thought of all the effort which had been made by Michel Platini and Gérard Houllier to help me, and of their confidence in me. I remembered the hopes that they nourished for their *enfant terrible*. I wanted to repay them now.

I'm not going to describe all the matches we played right up to the final game. However, the one we played on 5 April 1993 against Norwich City was extremely important and counted a great deal to our final victory.

Before that game the position in the league was as follows: Aston Villa were leaders, one point ahead of both United and Norwich, who were equal on points. It was clear that if we lost and Aston Villa won against Nottingham Forest, not only would they be four points ahead of us but Norwich would also profit from the result to take second place, leaving us in third position, three points behind them. As there were only six matches to play before the end of the season after this one, any slip-up would leave us in a very difficult position. It was imperative that we won.

In a nine-minute spell, Giggs, Kanchelskis and myself scored three goals early in the first half to ensure victory. Norwich did eventually pull back a

goal in the second half but it was not enough. This result gave us great confidence. It was a memorable victory for Manchester United. Hope remains eternal, but there can also be doubts. But not for very long, because we went on to win our last six matches.

In England I discovered another world, one of total relaxation in the dressing rooms only a few minutes before the kick-off for a big match. The foreigner who takes the risk of observing his English team-mates preparing for a game is going to be greatly surprised. I have never seen anything like it. The contrast with French players before an important match could not be more marked. I'm not judging which is better, I'm simply observing. It strikes me that in France a footballer rarely has a smile on his face. He wears a mask. From entering the dressing room an hour or two before kick-off, he is already playing the match, concentrated, tense, under pressure. For ten years my head and my body have been used to such a scenario before a big game.

In England the build-up is different. The players and management are calm and relaxed – a personification of the legendary British composure. The match has already been carefully prepared, discussed at training, so when we come to the stadium it's to play. No more questions about tactics and pressure, just a few words – 'That's it lads, and now it's up to us.' It is only just before kick-off that the mood changes. The joking and laughing stop; the Reds are no longer smiling. The signal is given and at one fell swoop the players line up in the tunnel which leads to the pitch, looking straight ahead of them, concentrated. In France we have an old proverb which reflects this approach: 'Before time is not the time, nor is it time after the time'. As soon as the team leaves the dressing room the match has started.

This difference of approach can be explained by the differences in education between the two countries. In Great Britain they acquire a sense of self-confidence and assurance very early on.

My son, Raphaël, is five. He goes to a typical English school. And I can see that at the school they have a way of encouraging the children to develop and to take on responsibility and to respect traditions. Here, there is much less hugging and kissing and fewer outbursts of emotion, and still far less moaning and groaning. The child is considered to be a person you have to help and encourage to stand on his own two feet.

That is the fighting spirit, the spirit of conquest if you like, which has made the reputation of English players; this impression of invincibility which they show and their tremendous pride when it's a question of defending their colours or defending the crown; the respect they show towards the referee – all these things are a product of an education where loyalty and devotion to one's friends are the key words.

◀ *The match against Norwich on 5 April 1993 was crucial. United won 3-1.* (Colorsport)

In England there are few training centres for potential professional footballers. The young players are recruited by the clubs and live in lodgings or at home and come every day to train with us. They must serve their apprenticeship in the natural environment of football. They learn to act independently. Nobody tells them what time they must go to bed nor what they must eat, as is the case with us in our football schools. The only things which are required in this relative autonomy is that, once at the stadium, the rules are very strict. They have to be keen, serious, well turned-out, well motivated, and that's all that's asked of them. The rest depends on them. In France, the young players live together at the club's football centre, similar to a miniature Lilleshall, and are subjected to great control, discipline and supervision.

It's very hard for somebody at the age of 15 to find within himself the strength to succeed and to make those sacrifices which are necessary if you want to be the best. However, I am sure that an English youth is used to taking the reins into his own hands and would be unhappy if he was shut in some kind of centre, as they are in France. Similarly, a young French player would, without doubt, feel himself abandoned and lost if he was in the English system.

Each country has a different way of training its young players. Whatever the case, whatever solutions are proffered, there is no miracle. One cannot forget that, ultimately, the place of truth for an athlete is, and will always be, the stadium.

Each match in the course of this mad season which I had the chance to experience was to constitute a test of nerves for the directors, management and players of Manchester United, different to what happened at Leeds. This was because a quarter of a century had passed without the national title.

For 26 years Manchester United had pursued their dream of being champions of England. Bryan Robson, the club captain and for so long the team's inspiration, was in his 12th season at Old Trafford – and was still waiting. Waiting for what? Waiting for that madness that would engulf the city; waiting for the moment when Old Trafford would again become the theatre of dreams which Bobby Charlton never ceased talking about. It's not easy to find the *mots justes* to describe how important the search for the title was to United.

Certainly, I had realised that Manchester United, thanks to its history and the heroes of the 1960s, was far more than a mere football club in the north of England. But I had never imagined such delight.

In Manchester the public is faithful, married for eternity to its players. As we entered the final straight towards the title, I saw this crowd overcome with pleasure at Crystal Palace after our 2-0 victory. As I was going towards the dressing room, a man of about 40 years of age came up to me and said: 'You know, Eric, for 26 years now, thousands of us have been coming to the ground each week waiting for this moment. There were 8,000 of us today at Crystal Palace, but there will be 500,000 of us in the streets of the city on 3 May if you beat Blackburn and bring back the title.'

What is so marvellous about the fans here is that they are not fair-weather spectators. Whatever the circumstances, they are always ready to enthuse about a piece of ball control, a touch, a swerve, a header into the corner. They know their football and they want to see it played as it should be.

'If you win the fight, you win the ball. If you win the ball, you win the game.' How many times did I hear Howard Wilkinson repeat those words at Leeds? I have never forgotten them, but with Manchester United we were going further, much further.

In England they play football which is at once spectacular and strong, technical and physical. You've got to run and suffer so that you earn your breaks and holidays, but pleasure and satisfaction are also considered to be very important.

Nothing was going to stop us from gaining our final triumph, certainly not the stupid injury I picked up against Sheffield Wednesday when I fractured the scaphoid of my wrist, nor the frustration of Bryan Robson on the substitutes' bench. Out of action for several months because of injury, the former captain of England was coming back to form and full fitness at the end of the season. Against Sheffield Wednesday, Bryan came on when we were losing 1-0 at Old Trafford.

Cantona looks on as Steve Bruce heads the winning goal past Sheffield Wednesday's goalkeeper Chris Woods.
(Colorsport)

Robson brought some order to the proceedings. With all our might, and in an atmosphere of collective hysteria, Steve Bruce headed in two goals in the last minutes of the game, the second well into stoppage time.

A week later, it was quite natural to expect that Ferguson would put Robson back in the team. We were playing at Coventry. Ferguson was in two minds about changing the side, but Robson came up and said to him: 'Leave the team as it is. Everything's going well. Don't make any changes.' On the next morning the newspapers drew attention to this final sacrifice of captain Robson.

We had won at Norwich, beaten Chelsea 3-0 and triumphed over Palace 2-0. So, as the season reached its climax, I could go to Paris in a good state of mind to prepare for France's next international.

On Saturday 24 April at midday I met up with the rest of the national team and Gérard Houllier, the manager. We were preparing for the game against Sweden on the long qualifying road to the World Cup. Afterwards, I would return for the crunch match with Blackburn on 3 May. This was a marvellous programme to look forward to before the end of the season and the holidays.

It is 28 April 1993, the day of the match. My clothes, which I had hastily put on in the dressing room of the Parc des Princes, were wet through by a warm and fresh rain. It was dark, but the streets glistened in the downpour as the heavens opened.

It's marvellous to be a top-level sportsman on such an occasion and to realise that with the exception of a few things which didn't come off, a couple of hesitations in front of goal, you've given everything, you've tried everything. If there's a God above looking at us, he certainly didn't forget me that evening.

In France we say that an individual who never asks any questions is a happy idiot. That evening I was the king of idiots because my pleasure didn't come simply from the two goals I had just scored. The pleasure was greater than that. It came from the huge stands from which the fans shouted my name after the second goal. We carried their joy off the field with us and brought it into the dressing room to join the players who are drenched with the ecstasy of victory. The pleasure came with us to the shower; it was in my clothes; it came along with us to the table which we had reserved in a small nightclub in Paris. There, nobody can deceive anybody, nobody can be mistaken. Those at my table are my friends.

We knew quite well that the France versus Sweden match wouldn't be a walkover. The images and impressions of that afternoon return to my mind: the heat of the pitch, the heat of the Parc des Princes, was stifling. After quarter of an hour I was wet with sweat. I was also anxious, because Dahlin had profited from a misunderstanding in our defence to score the first goal and I was especially anxious about the way the game was going. The Swedes had adopted a square defence and we found that we were incapable of breaching it.

The greatest of football's technicians, from Cruyff to Platini and including Franz Beckenbauer, insist on the fact that you have to look around before touching the ball. It wasn't by chance that the penalty which we finally earned came as a result of a collective piece of one-touch football. The Swedish lock was at last broken. The ball was mine. It was a penalty and I had to take it.

For a player whose avowed objective on the field in the World Cup, just as in a training session, is to try out moves, short dribbles, pieces of control, bending the ball or other improvisations, shooting at goal is the most formidable test of truth. The penalty kick is the most fearsome of actions, but it is easy to execute. I enjoy this moment that holds all those who are watching in suspense. It's terrible, with the executioner face to face with his victim. Fifteen seconds punctuated by a flash of lightning. The crowd explodes or crumbles. The penalty is either happiness or sadness, nothing else.

I put the ball on the spot and scored. Then, in the 85th minute, I discovered that discreet charm which is enjoyed by goal poachers. A moment's inattention by the man who was marking me and I dive in and the score eloquently tells the story: 2-1 in our favour.

It's all over.

And then it all begins again. I returned to England the following morning, where I tried to get a bit of rest, perhaps only a couple of hours. I decided not to stay up late that evening. The champagne could come later. On Monday 3 May, for example, we could be champions of England.

I caught the first plane to Manchester at seven o'clock in the morning and it was easy to imagine that this might be a flight to glory. A celebration more radiant, perhaps, than the one we enjoyed at Leeds is waiting for me with my comrades at Manchester United. Just like me, most of the players will not have slept, or would have slept very little, because they have all been on international duty taking part in qualifying matches for the 1994 World Cup.

When the news reached Manchester, it would have made the vocal cords of Simply Red's Mick Hucknall (himself a big United fan) throb, for on Sunday 2 May the main headline on the evening television news was: Aston Villa had been beaten 1-0 at Oldham and were therefore unable to catch Manchester United. Nick Henry, the scorer of the Oldham goal, could not have had any doubts about the commotion which he would unleash by beating the Villa goalkeeper.

We are the champions!

Lying on my bed in my hotel in Manchester, I admit that it was hard for me to appreciate what was really happening. Others could do so without difficulty. The supporters had already invaded the centre of the town; Albert Square had become one long red river of flags and banners. Everybody was in the street. Piccadilly was in turmoil and it would be a bold man who tried to count how many pints of beer were sunk that evening.

Sometimes this red wave, when it rolls towards Old Trafford, makes me afraid. But not this time. This evening one must live and enjoy the moment with my team-mates.

It's nine o'clock; the telephone is going non-stop. Everyone is excited, but I must somehow find the time to concentrate sufficiently for our last home match of the season. Steve Bruce has just called me.

'Congratulations, Eric. Come along to my house this evening. We're going to celebrate the title.'

In saying that, Bruce laughed and it was the sort of laugh that explained the nature of such an invitation. In the taxi which took me to Bramhall, where Bruce lives, the memories of a fabulous week unfolded in my mind. What a week! What madness! Success against the Swedes in the Parc des Princes and now champions of England with United.

When I arrived at Steve Bruce's house, the song 'We Are The Champions' was playing. We will hear the voice of Freddie Mercury again some hours later and his song will be taken up by over 40,000 spectators.

In the principal room which opens onto the garden there is a celebration. Everyone's there, all my team-mates from United. Obviously, I can't swear eternal fidelity and loyalty but, as long as we stay together, I am convinced that we will be able to move mountains. 'I'm over the moon,' commented Sir Matt Busby, the manager who created the legend that is Manchester United, when he heard that we had won the title. We all feel ready to make further trips to the moon, providing that the ship that takes us there is as joyful and free as this one.

Bryan Robson was there too. This man, who captained England for so long throughout the 1980s, is loved by all the fans of Manchester United. It's very interesting to hear the crowd at Old Trafford chant even when Bryan is going to warm up. The public there don't forget those who have made them dream.

The crowd sings in the joy of victory and pain of defeat – at Old Trafford just as at Anfield, Elland Road and Ibrox. Football is perhaps the only spectacle which is able to create a free and intense social relationship. Nobody is forced to come to the stadium. Nobody is forced to sing. But it's as if everything had been planned and prepared when thousands of hearts let themselves be heard and sing to each other.

Steve Bruce had just put dozens of beers and as many bottles of champagne on his bar when, just after midnight, Kanchelskis arrived. Finally, the full team is there. What price would our supporters have paid just to be with us at our improvised celebration? In one movement we were all drinking to the victory. A page of history in British football had just been made.

It's late. Outside the Manchester sky is full of stars. Tomorrow will be fine at Old Trafford. 'And in front of Michel Platini,' says Steve Bruce proudly, referring to tomorrow's match.

We had come a full circle. Michel Platini, who had put my English raincoat on my back 14 months earlier, would be in the stands alongside Gérard Houllier and the two Jean-Jacques (Bertrand and Amorfini). In the space of a few hours my greatest hopes and joys would come together in the same place. The happiness of a second title in England (the third consecutive one if you count Marseille, as a friend pointed out to me, with a twinkle in his eye) and above all the pride of not disappointing the hopes of my former international manager and the plans of the Blues' new manager. Finally, I was proud that I had maintained my liberty.

I didn't sleep well that night.

Undoubtedly, this was because I had only one thing on my mind and I could not forget it: to rejoin my team-mates at Old Trafford knowing that this day was going to give me the greatest sunshine of my career. I do not regret anything that I lived through in France. My travels and my breakdowns have made me more solid, but I don't look too closely at the past.

On the black market near the stadium, touts were selling tickets for £100 to £150 at the very least. An incredible communion between the public and the players is assured.

We had been crowned champions of England the day before by default, thanks to Oldham's victory. Now we wanted to play like champions. Our supporters had last seen us at home when we won 3-0 against Chelsea on 17 April, now they would see us again as champions. The lid was ready to jump off, mouths were ready to open. It was a feeling of the greatest delight and madness.

The songs that came from the depths of the crowd were so beautiful that for an instant I didn't want to have to play, but would have liked to stand still somewhere and just listen.

At quarter to seven, Steve Bruce led us out onto the pitch and the voice of the people became clearly heard. Blackburn still had a chance of getting to Europe and so we knew that they were going to try to make it a hard match. Kenny Dalglish even claimed that they were going to beat us.

The loudspeaker system had started with Queen's 'We Are The Champions' and now it was 'Simply The Best' by Tina Turner. After a few

With the Premiership title already won, United were able to put on the style against Blackburn Rovers in May 1993. (A. de Martignac/Presse-Sports)

'The songs that came from the depths of the crowd were so beautiful that for an instant I didn't want to have to play, but would have liked to stand still somewhere and just listen.' (Presse-Sports)

The celebrations continue to the strains of 'We Are The Champions'. Cantona is flanked by his interpreter, George Scanlan (right), and kit man Norman Davis. (Presse-Sports)

bars, it looked as if Paul Ince was going to start a dance on the field.

Alex Ferguson was entitled to hold on tight to his new honour: the Barclays Manager of the Month Award had been presented to him in the centre of the field. Although this was the highest point, he had had a whole series of ups and downs in recent years. It was he who had inherited the Red Army in November 1986 and he had twice previously taken Manchester United to second place.

But Manchester United were not created to be runners-up. The FA Cup in 1990, then the Cup-Winners' Cup the following year count among the honours which Ferguson has brought to Manchester. But the main one was the title.

Manchester will remember.

As expected, Kenny Dalglish's side made a fast start and scored in the seventh minute of the match through Gallacher, who slammed the ball into the near corner of the net from a pass from Sherwood.

What does it matter? The voices of Old Trafford soon find their tempo and they do not believe that one goal will be enough to beat us. 'Champions! Champions!' they shout. The spectators know how to count and their memory does not let them down. Manchester United have already scored almost 70 goals this season and a lot of disappointing starts have been changed by a goal in the last minutes.

Ryan Giggs proves that they have no need to worry when, less than a quarter of an hour after the opening goal, the young Welshman takes a free kick from 25 metres and deceives the goalkeeper. There is an explosion of joy in the stadium. Behind Mimms's goal the sky bursts and singing is heard in the four corners of the stadium. Blackburn have been floored. Kenny Dalglish's team won't get up again.

Paul Ince, who has no equal in causing havoc on the pitch, is everywhere. Giggs, bristling with insolence, takes on his man down the line, juggling the ball. Lee Sharpe, still only 21, shows his nonchalance as he creates so many holes in the Blackburn defence. He has made a remarkable recovery from the meningitis which kept him out of the game for so long. As for Steve Bruce, our heroic captain, the fact that he'd acted as wine waiter for us the night before didn't stop him in any way from getting hold of the ball or hitting some excellent long passes towards the Blackburn goal. Bruce is happy. That is obvious.

I am enjoying myself.

At half-time, Bryan Robson comes on for Lee Sharpe. And in the 62nd minute Mark Hughes gets the ball and gives it to me. I do just enough to pass it to Paul Ince for the second goal.

Everyone in the team had scored at least one goal in the course of the season. Everybody, that is, except Pallister. In the last seconds of the match, the referee whistles for a free kick 18 metres out. In order to complete our celebrations, we let Pallister take the free kick. He approaches the ball and, in the last minute of the last game at Old Trafford the last player not to have scored during the whole season shoots into the left-hand corner of the Blackburn goal. Three goals for Manchester United!

Bewitched, the crowd behind the Blackburn goal seems to crumble onto the turf.

Pallister was running like a jumping jack. Forty thousand spectators could be heard singing 'Glory, Glory, Man United…'

We brandish the cup before Sir Matt Busby, the man whose most beautiful children had perished in that air catastrophe. Although the joy is intense, those who win always end up thinking back to those players who were killed in that terrible disaster in 1958.

We do a slow lap of honour to the cheers from the Stretford End and all around the ground: 'Champions, champions…'

When I compare this spectacle to all the shows in the world, this one isn't far from being the most perfect because, just as in certain theatres, the audience is almost part of the play, so here you could almost imagine the spectators clapping and calling us back on stage just as they ask a singer to do an encore.

I went back into the dressing rooms. Some lads had managed to escape the vigilance of the police and came up to congratulate me. As ever, there was this wish to touch a player, to carry off something, to look at you. I protected my wrist because it was hurting and we still had another match away at Wimbledon.

This time, the champagne could flow all night. Everybody was there now, all the heroes of the Red Army, the young and the old.

My shower was long and enjoyable. I didn't go to the celebrations which were given in our honour by a supporter who owns a hotel in town. I wanted to get home to Leeds to be with my young son.

Chapter Nine

···

Always Look on the Bright Side of Life

*W*riting in January 1994, just after the death of Sir Matt Busby, Cantona *spoke of his hopes for the future. Already it is clear that he has settled in at United in a way that had eluded him at his other clubs – United has become a second family to him.*

I am at the end of my first year with Manchester United. So much has happened so quickly that I need time to catch my breath. In spite of two big disappointments in November, I am enjoying my football more than at any other time in my life. First, Manchester United were knocked out of the European Cup by Galatasaray on a passionate evening in Turkey; then France failed to win a place in the World Cup finals in the USA this coming summer, having set ourselves up to do just that. But France's failure to obtain the necessary one point to qualify from two home matches against Israel and Bulgaria will serve as a lesson to anyone who thinks that the race is won or the tape is broken until it has actually happened. So it is with Manchester United, as we go into the new year of 1994: we must make sure that we take nothing for granted, even though the bookies are convinced that we must win the league. I shall certainly be training and practising with great diligence and keenness to enable me to be in top form for each game.

Our club and our supporters deserve the best, and that is what I intend to serve up. Watching football is an expensive hobby and my objective is to provide as much pleasure and enjoyment as possible to all our fans so that they can take home with them some warm memories of our play.

Manchester United is the best and most consistent team I have played for over a period of time. Although any team can be capable of greatness in a particular match, it is the ability to maintain it that marks out this team. Some of our performances this year have been outstanding and I always get great satisfaction from our play and our victories, which depend on all of us and not just on one or two players as the press will often have you believe.

This season, as you know, started extremely well for United without me when I was unable to play because of injury. Our display in beating Arsenal in the Charity Shield gave some indication of our potential for the present season and I was delighted to return to a side which had already secured three wins and a draw in the first four matches of the present campaign.

My first game back was, for me personally as well as for the team, a great success. We beat Southampton 3-1 at The Dell and I scored by lobbing the ball over Tim Flowers, who was soon to become the world's most expensive goalkeeper when he signed for Blackburn Rovers.

After a surprise defeat by Chelsea on 11 September, we were not to be beaten again in the league for the rest of 1993, and we began a run of victories that saw our lead over the rest of the Premiership keep on growing.

The match against Arsenal, one of our greatest rivals, saw the two teams cancel out each other. However, I managed to score the only goal of the game from a free kick, so we could at least be happy that we had won.

Our derby match against Manchester City, however, was a thriller. The game came only days after we had lost out to Galatasaray and the press had

7 November 1993: Cantona scores the first of his two goals against Manchester City in a thrilling derby match. (Colorsport)

been quick to suggest that our golden run might be over. They recalled how Leeds United had fallen away after losing to Glasgow Rangers the previous year – this was, they told us, a crucial match. But Manchester have a much stronger squad, and the spirit in the team is magnificent. We were to need it, because we go in at half time 2-0 down.

Manager Alex Ferguson tells us we cannot let it slip now, especially as half of Manchester is waiting for us to fall and will not let us forget it if we do. I play much deeper in the second half, and we begin to play much better. We are sweeping forward. We will not be stopped today. I score two goals to draw us level. I run to the fans massed behind the goal to celebrate. They sense that we will win and they are happy because it is worse to lose to City than anyone else. They are right and Roy Keane scores the winner with two minutes to go. We had proved that we could recover from the disappointments of Europe.

On the first anniversary of my arrival at Old Trafford, we go to Coventry City and I celebrate by scoring the only goal of the game. Someone tells me that we have now won 31 out of the 42 league matches we have played since I arrived.

The Christmas period is always a busy one in English football, and this year we played five games in 16 days. Our first opponents were Aston Villa,

Cantona scores another two in United's Christmas encounter with Aston Villa. (Empics)

◄ *He kisses the red jersey of Manchester United in celebration of the amazing comeback he has orchestrated.* (Colorsport)

who challenged us for so long last season, but at Old Trafford they lose 3-1 and I give the fans two goals to take my total for the season to 13. It is my Christmas present to them.

There is little time for Christmas with Isabelle and Raphaël, because, on Boxing Day, Blackburn Rovers, another strong side, are our visitors. It is a full house once again, over 44,000 spectators are packed into Old Trafford. Their cheers and their singing encourage us after we fall a goal behind. The whole team is now at one with the supporters. Together we cannot lose.

With seconds left, we have a corner. Even Peter Schmeichel is in the penalty area. The ball comes over. There is a scramble. Paul Ince scores. We *will* not lose.

Oldham are beaten 5-2 in a splendid display of attacking football, and then my old club Leeds comes to the home of the Red Devils. We cannot score, but they do not look like they will ever do so. No goals, but the game against Liverpool at Anfield will make up for that.

It was the first time that I had played in this fixture between the two great sides. I had thought the rivalry between Manchester United and Leeds or Manchester City was intense, but this was possibly even more dramatic. Anfield is red with the colours of both sets of supporters. The atmosphere is charged with emotion and, as we go onto the field, the smell of fireworks and drifting smoke add mystery and suspense to the evening. There is something unusual and unnatural in the air; you feel that something out of the ordinary is going to happen.

Suddenly, the Kop is silenced to the point of disbelief as we score three goals in the first 25 minutes. But Liverpool will not lie down. The game is played with passion and fire. This is entertainment. Blink and you might miss a goal.

The final score is 3-3. This is fair because neither side deserves to lose. Although I am disappointed that we have let the game slip, the crowd had got their money's worth, and their loyalty and commitment to their teams had not gone unrewarded.

This is the essence of British football – the unexpected, 90 minutes of cut and thrust, a refusal to give in, goalmouth incidents, a belief that the best way to defend is to attack, an absence of malice and pretence, high levels of sportsmanship on the field and in the crowd, in spite of the fierce rivalry between Liverpool and United. In this match the only victor is football and our love of the game.

Having played in such a game at Anfield I now appreciate why the players and the fans of Saint-Etienne look back on their European Cup game there in 1977 with such affection and warmth, even though they lost to a late goal by super-sub David Fairclough.

Cantona, the family man. (Empics)

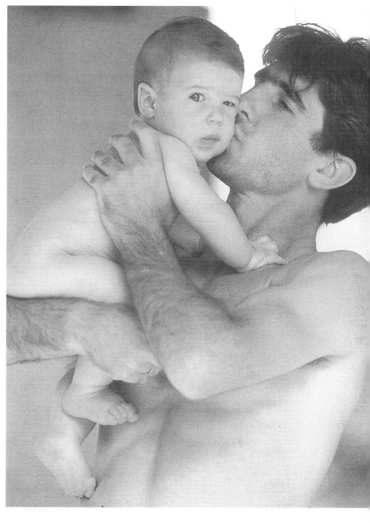

It was, in fact, my 50th match for Manchester United. During that time, the team has played so well that we have lost only two games. I am pleased that I have managed to score 23 goals in that period.

I am a family man and Manchester United have made me feel part of their huge family. It is a cosmopolitan team – Welsh, Danish, Scottish, Irish, French, Ukrainian as well as English – but there is a fraternal link.

It is not easy for any new player to adapt to the requirements of such a club where the spectres of Best, Charlton, Law, Stiles, Crerand, Busby and others still hover and where the public have seen the very best of football. It can be particularly hard for a foreigner without full knowledge of the language to settle into such surroundings. It is so easy to be left in the dark, to half understand what is being said.

Alex Ferguson, lover of France though he is, does not have pretensions to be able to speak fluent French and is conscious of my need to be fully informed. Therefore a quick meeting between Alex, my interpreter George Scanlan and myself at the Cliff, Old Trafford or in the hotel before an away game has usually been enough to iron out any potential difficulty. In such a way, just before Christmas, Alex called me to his office and told me that I was being followed. How life never changes! There will always be little shits who are attempting to dig up dirt, even where it does not exist.

A journalist and his photographer had been following me wherever I went. They wanted to catch me in the arms of a player's wife because rumour had been rife that I was having an affair with her when I was playing for Leeds.

Some even thought this was the main reason that Leeds United had to part company with me. What malicious nonsense! How low are people prepared to stoop?

Anyhow these two, for whom there is only one word – shits – had been following me. When I had been told about it, I noticed that I was being tailed by a maroon Mini Austin in which a large fat man was squeezed into the passenger seat. It was enough to make you laugh. The driver gave the impression that he had no idea where he was going. To make life harder for him, I turned without making any signals, stopped and re-started, got into dense traffic, changed lanes and, in all sorts of manoeuvres tried to throw them off the scent. But these two idiots continued to track me and I could see them in my mirror trying to act as if everything was normal. I was in pain with laughter!

I found out that a newspaper had asked a French journalist for the sum of £15,000 to dig up some sex intrigues which they could pin on me. Needless to say, in spite of all their wasted efforts, the newspaper could find nothing of the kind and the papers continued to write about me only in football terms.

Such attempts to unsettle me have been few while I have been in England. The press have left me in peace to concentrate on my football, but the club has shown its readiness to protect my interests should they be threatened. For example, in February 1993, shortly before the game with Leeds, a journalist from the *Daily Express* approached me with a request for an interview. In spite of my refusal, the paper went ahead and published a series of three long pieces on me, clearly intended to be based on exclusive interviews with the newspaper.

The club solicitor, Maurice Watkins, met George Scanlan and myself in his offices and came to the conclusion that the interviews, which had not taken place, portrayed me in a poor light and that remarks which I was alleged to have made about my time at Leeds could easily stir up hostility towards me when we played at Elland Road. The speedy action of the club's solicitors not only resulted in the newspaper having to pay damages, but has also prevented any other newspapers taking similar liberties.

It is comforting to know that the club is on my side. In the only other incident of note, in the match against Galatasaray, the English newspapers implied that I had been sent off at the end of the game for being stupid enough to criticise the French-speaking Swiss referee in French. Again Maurice Watkins, Alex Ferguson and George met to discuss the matter and once again my version of events was accepted.

In fact, I did not speak to the referee. I simply went up to shake his hand and indicated with my fingers that his rating for the match was zero. I turned and went away, not even realising that he had produced the red card. For this action, I was banned from four games in European competition. But the Swiss referee had demanded much greater punishment, and without the support of Manchester United he might have succeeded in his wish.

What annoyed me most of all is that I was hit on the head with a truncheon by a Turkish policeman, the sort of fellow who sends you to prison for being out of work, or when you are hungry and you go and steal a bar of chocolate from the supermarket. He was the sort of bloke who thinks the world revolves around him when he's in uniform. Even dressed up like that, he has not the courage to act face-to-face but prefers to strike from behind.

Of course, I was upset at being knocked out of the European Cup, at the spoiling tactics of the opponents, at the fact that no stoppage time was added, and by being given the red card after the game had ended. But, above all, I had been hit from behind by that shit of a Turkish policeman. Maybe we'll bump into each other again some time!

I must say that since I have been in England I have never had any problems with referees. Firstly, they are the best, because they are less theatrical and not concerned about being the stars on the field. Secondly, they go about their job quietly and seriously. They referee honestly. You don't feel that they are corrupt as is sometimes the case elsewhere. They may make mistakes from time to time, but they are honest mistakes like we all make.

In spite of these isolated incidents that I have mentioned above, everything has been fine at Manchester United. The road is long, but I dream of winning a second successive championship medal with the club. Scarcely has my dream commenced when another match approaches, and another, and then another. It is an infernal rhythm in which you have to have proper rest. You must concentrate your mind so that you are in perfect shape and form to make others dream about you. But there is no time to dream yourself. You have to prepare for the future by living the present with great intensity. Just before the game I see everything in my head. In my mind's eye, I anticipate what I'll do with the ball, what positions I will take up. This helps me to concentrate. I imagine the ball to be alive, sensitive and responding to the touch of my foot, to my caresses, just like a woman with the man she loves. Perhaps that is utopia and can never be exactly true, but it helps me in my attempt to explain to you my love and affection for the ball.

In England I hear now and again, and especially since all the British international teams failed to qualify for the finals of the World Cup in America in 1994, that the players of the future must have more technical ability and be more creative than they are now. There are experienced players with these qualities, but what is most encouraging is the arrival on the scene of young players with great talent, like Barmby, Fowler and Anderton.

You will reply that perhaps there are too few of them and I will respond that a great team does not necessarily consist of the best players. In a great team there are players who complement each other – the workers, the creators and the goalscorers. The workers work with the creators who, in their turn, create for the goalscorers. And rest assured that England has enough of all three categories. Having said that, why weren't the creative players called up for the qualifying matches? Gascoigne would not have felt so alone; Ince and Pallister would have known who they were working for; and with such support Ian Wright would have shown that he can score goals at international level with the same frequency as he achieves at club level.

What a shame that England and France will be watching the finals on television. How I personally regret that France could not get that tiny point from two home games, even losing the last match against Bulgaria 15 seconds from the final whistle. I would have wanted not only to participate, but to show that France is one of the best teams in the world.

Now everything rests ahead of us. Manchester United must make sure that we win the Premiership this year, so that once again we will have the chance to play in Europe and make another attempt at winning the coveted prize of the European Cup. That would have made Sir Matt Busby extremely happy, I know, and we will do our best to achieve that goal.

I will say a few words about the football family which I work with each day. The head of that family is Alex Ferguson, to whom I am grateful for signing me on for Manchester United, knowing the risk he might have been taking if he had believed all the tales he had heard about me. Alex Ferguson has enjoyed a magnificent career as a player and manager, although when he advises me about the rights and wrongs of retaliation he lets slip that he has been sent off more times than I have. 'Determination' is a word which he frequently uses in his team talks, which give a full analysis of the other team. After such pre-match talks, you always feel encouraged and feel that you have a good chance of winning.

'Look around at yourselves and remember what a good team you belong to. The only way you are going to lose is if you decide to beat yourselves. Patience, determination, good passing and movement, don't give the ball away and let's see some fire, especially in the last third of the field. Above all, go out and enjoy yourselves. If you can't enjoy playing in this team, you'll never enjoy playing anywhere. Good luck, lads.'

He is the boss. He is a lover of football, someone who would be watching boys playing in the rain if he did not happen to be manager of the biggest club in Britain. After the match he will eagerly await all the results on television, from the Premiership to all the non-League results. The only time when he is not thinking about football is on the bus to and from away games when he is playing cards with Gary Pallister, Bryan Robson and Steve Bruce. I understand from them that he is as determined to win at cards as he is at football.

When I am driving to Manchester to train, I look forward with eager anticipation to the sessions of Brian Kidd, our coach. I am happy because, at some clubs, the training sessions have not been of any interest. But there are coaches like Kiddo who make you want to train and he gives you a lift, he motivates you. What a joy it is to train under him with the ball all the time for physical and technical work, passing, shooting and small games.

You feel that he has meticulously prepared everything and sometimes he calls George and myself over to ask my reaction to this or that exercise or session. There is more than quality in what he does. There is love, and you

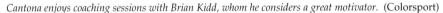

Cantona enjoys coaching sessions with Brian Kidd, whom he considers a great motivator. (Colorsport)

can quickly see that he has been a great player. Brian Kidd began his football career at Manchester United and, at the age of 18, played with the likes of Best and Charlton in the 1968 European Cup-winning team. A glittering career with United, Manchester City, Arsenal, Everton and then in the newly formed American league has not made him swollen-headed. He is down-to-earth, pragmatic and modest. He is still slightly embarrassed at seeing those television pictures of him and Alex Ferguson racing onto the pitch to celebrate the unforgettable winning goal from Steve Bruce against Sheffield Wednesday in the ninth minute of extra time in April last year. It was a key victory in our road to the Championship last season. He still does a five-mile cross-country run after training to keep himself fit, and there are many supporters who go to the games early just to see the accuracy of his kicking when he warms up Peter Schmeichel before kick-off.

Two other key members of the first-team staff are Jimmy McGregor, the physio, and Norman Davis, the kit man. Jimmy is very experienced and very quick to see an injury on the field almost before it's happened. He has been a great help to me when I broke my scaphoid and when I had some hamstring trouble. He is accurate in diagnosis and has the habit of closing his eyes when feeling for the source of injury, a habit he developed in his early days when he did his training with a blind sports physiotherapist in Scotland. Both Jimmy and Norman have made every effort to make me feel at home, and I am grateful for the way they look after me.

Of course, the other person with us all the time is George Scanlan, who interprets for Andrei Kanchelskis and myself. He is knowledgeable about football and observes with a professional eye. He has been a big help to Andrei and myself on and off the field, ensuring that we know precisely what is happening.

Because most of the side have been playing together for a few years, and they know each other well and trust one another on the pitch, team spirit is high and the relationship between all the players is excellent. They have all played their part in making me feel welcome and have been ready to support me in the free role which Alex Ferguson has given me. I am conscious of the work that they do on my behalf.

Manchester United have believed in me and there is no greater source of confidence and inspiration for a player than the knowledge that people believe in you. The one or two specialists who may have had doubts about me had obviously swallowed the image which certain people at Leeds may have wished to create when I switched from white to red.

On a lighter note, I was amused to read the following attempts to win the poetry prize recently awarded by United's official magazine. Here are two poems which caught my eye:

Poetry in Motion
He struts around the field of play
Like a Spanish matador.
In the arena that's known as the Stadium of
    Dreams
He majestically takes the floor.
He's larger than life
And brimming with passion.
Typically French, full of life
An eye for fashion.
When he's on the pitch he makes things happen
With a flair we've come to love.
He's got natural talent and grace beyond words,
One might say a gift from above.
He came from across the Pennines,
Changing from white to red.
Their loss is our gain – what's his name?
Cantona.

Une autre perspective
Some see you from a distance, admire you from
    afar.
To them you're just that Frenchman, that Eric
    Cantona.
I wish I could be like them, admiring only skill
Instead of wanting more than just magnificent
    goalmouth thrills.
Your intelligence alarms me, so rare in such
    a trade.
Your sultry gaze unnerves me, it could easily
    persuade.
Should you ever be in need, *cher*, of company
    at the bar
Please let me bring new meaning to that famous
    chant 'Ooh, ah'!

Poetry in motion. (Empics)

129

The winning poem was written in French by a young lady in Leamington Spa who had gone to watch us beat Coventry 5-0 at Old Trafford. She describes waiting in the queue to buy a ticket for the match when I turned up for the game. She asked me to autograph her scarf, because she didn't have any paper. When the pen wouldn't work on the cloth, she asked me to write on the palm of her hand, 'sur la palme il a écrit, une grande occasion dans ma vie'. She also said that I forgot to give her pen back!

It is thrilling to know the warmth of support which I enjoy here in Manchester and elsewhere in England, but we must all remember that, however famous we are, we are really nothing, just a drop of water in the ocean and the earth won't stop revolving when we have gone.

I feel very much part of a big, happy, supportive family. Having read about my own childhood and my own parents and the mutual affection which we enjoyed, you will see how important the notion of family is to me. After all the ups and downs in my football career, it is a small miracle that I have managed to find such contentment here in a foreign country. I value truth, honesty, respect for one another, sincerity, compassion and understanding. These qualities are found at Manchester United.

It has been a year of happiness here. A year you could only dream about. Isabelle continues to enjoy her work teaching French at Leeds University and Raphaël is making progress with his English at school. We are all extremely happy, and the team continues to win. Victory is a friend, a friend you must not betray.

As I prepare to draw the curtains on my book and concentrate my thoughts on the match with Everton on Saturday, I am sad to hear the news of the death of the father of the Manchester United family, Sir Matt Busby. As you will know, his name appears several times in this book.

Nobody can ever write or speak about Manchester United without mentioning his name. You sense and feel that his blood runs through every vein of the club's body. His name is engraved in the hearts of all those who love beautiful football. His kindness, courage, gentility and resilience serve as an inspiration and example to everybody.

His legacy of playing with style – win, lose or draw – will be preserved. His ideals, principles and beliefs will not be forgotten. I am pleased that I played in front of him, and that he lived to see United champions once more.

Chapter Ten

· ·

Bring on the Double

Having completed the 1994 Double, Cantona knew that the side still had to prove itself in Europe – an aim he still cherishes to this day. It was during the second part of the 1993–4 season that questions began to be asked about his (and the team's) disciplinary record, but it was the good that outweighed the bad for him and for the fans.

By the end of January 1994, it was a two-horse race for the biggest prize in English football – the Premiership title. Alex Ferguson stressed that this was our number one objective, even though we had begun to have good runs in both the Coca-Cola Cup and the FA Cup. My dream was to win all three and to set a record which has not been achieved in English football. It was a dream that so nearly came true.

I picked up an injury in the 2-2 draw against West Ham United at the end of February. Beforehand, the team had received a hostile reception from the Upton Park crowd, but it was Paul Ince who was especially singled out. Their fans had not forgiven him for leaving the club and for being photographed in a Manchester United shirt before the deal had gone through. Surprisingly, though he had been at Old Trafford for well over four years, it was his first game back at his old club. As the coach drew close to the ground, we noticed workmen digging a huge hole and Brian McClair yelled out: 'They're getting your grave ready for you, Paul.'

This sort of comment is typical of the camaraderie and good humour of the United squad. It was a potentially tense occasion, and the pressure on Paul Ince in particular could have become great, so it was important that we did not let it get to us. Indeed, as the pressure on the side mounted during the rest of the season, it was this team spirit and the ability to relax that was to help pull us through.

The injury caused me to miss the next two games, one of which was the second leg of the Coca-Cola Cup semi-final against Sheffield Wednesday at Hillsborough. We had gone into the match with a 1-0 lead after the tie at Old

Trafford and it was a potentially difficult fixture. Watching the team in action from my seat in the stands I was very impressed with what I saw. We won 4-1 thanks to goals from my replacement Brian McClair, two from Mark Hughes and another from Andrei Kanchelskis.

But all did not go so well in the second game, against Chelsea at Old Trafford. They had beaten us 1-0 earlier in the season, but we had not lost at home for 17 months and had also gone 34 matches undefeated. The game was to show conclusively that reputations and records count for nothing in football as Chelsea again beat us 1-0. By now, questions were being asked of us: had we lost our way? Blackburn were closing in on us and many thought that the difficulty of trying to win three trophies might prove too much.

Our next game was in the FA Cup against Charlton Athletic for a place in the semi-final. This season had already proved one for major upsets in the competition, with top teams regularly falling to sides from the lower divisions. Indeed, Charlton had already beaten Blackburn on their way to reaching the sixth round. For a while it looked as though they might manage to triumph over both of the top two sides, especially when Peter Schmeichel was sent off just on the stroke of half-time.

The break gave us time to collect our thoughts and to plan our escape. Les Sealey went in goal and the boss was thinking of taking off Mark Hughes until Brian Kidd said that such a move would give us less flexibility. In the end, the boss asked me to play up front on my own between Ryan and Andrei, with Mark joining Paul Ince in midfield and Roy Keane moving into Paul Parker's place at right back. The second half display was to serve as another example of the spirit and courage which exist at Old Trafford, and the 3-1 victory will be remembered as an important step towards Wembley.

If that was a performance of courage, our next game – against Sheffield Wednesday, hungry for revenge – was to show the team in complete harmony, each player in perfect tune with his team-mate.

The hail storm is turning the pitch white and slippery, but it cannot prevent a performance of extraordinary brilliance in which everyone shows the highest levels of passing, movement and shooting. We win 5-0 and go seven points clear of Blackburn. An injury to Andrei Kanchelskis is the only flaw in the evening.

The next two games were not so happy, for the team or for me. We drew 2-2 at both Swindon and Arsenal, and I was shown the red card in both matches. Against Swindon I could have no complaints with the referee's decision, although I am certain that my rubber studs would have caused little discomfort to John Moncur. Ironically, he told me that he had voted for me in the PFA Player of the Year award, due to be announced soon after.

The second sending-off, against Arsenal, was not merited. I had just received a yellow card for a foul tackle on Ian Selley, and I cannot argue with that decision. The red card came a couple of minutes later for a supposed dangerous tackle on Tony Adams just before the end of the game. It was a travesty of justice. Players close to the incident were outraged, for I had simply jumped over Adams to avoid a clash, conscious of the fact that I had already been cautioned and that a second sending-off would mean that I would miss several games. I was astonished to see the referee waving a red card at me, but I walked straight off while my team-mates protested and the travelling United fans howled at the referee.

The television pictures, shown so often, were to prove that I should not have been sent off. Both Paul Merson and Tony Adams were generous enough to state to the press that the decision was wrong. Anyone can make a mistake, and I would never be overcritical of someone for doing so. However, if I make a mistake, I am ashamed if I fail to admit it.

I expressed such sentiments after the match to correspondents from *l'Equipe*, and the next day the comments had been translated and appeared in all the English newspapers. In France, we are allowed to make such observations about the referees, and all I was saying was that he should have been man enough to admit that he had made a mistake. Such an admission would have enhanced his reputation. Instead of concentrating on the obvious error of judgement on the part of the referee, the Football Association was to tackle me over the comments that I had made.

The five-match ban I received for the two sendings-off could not have come at a worse time for me and the team. I think that this distraction may have had something to do with the defeat against Aston Villa in the Coca-Cola Cup final at Wembley. Although I had played on this wonderful surface before, this was my first final at the ground. With nearly 80,000 fans chanting for the teams, it was a remarkable day, and I will never forget the astonishing support I received from the United fans as I came out to warm up for the game. It meant so much to me after a difficult week, and I hoped that I could help give them the prize they wanted.

We did not play badly, but things did not go our way. The third goal they scored summed up the whole day. Not only was it the final nail in our coffin, but Andrei was sent off – the punishment being out of all proportion to the crime. It was one of those occasions when the rules should allow a referee to use his discretion in the name of fairness and good sense. Within a few games, all three of United's foreign players had been sent off.

The critics were now convinced that United's season was falling apart. Before the final, the talk had been that we could win a unique treble, now the press believed we could end up with nothing. For us it was the moment to take stock of the situation, not to panic but to regain the composure and the courage that we had shown all season. All great teams have their ups and downs, but the truly great teams are always capable of coming back and overcoming adversity. The next six weeks would show whether we had the self-belief to be real champions.

Unconvincing home wins over Liverpool and Oldham and an away defeat at Blackburn provided ammunition for the sceptics. But then footballing fate and destiny took a hand. As I watched the clock ticking away in the Wembley semi-final against Oldham, with United 1-0 down and only 45 seconds of extra time remaining, there seemed to be no chance. A miracle was needed. It came with Mark Hughes' outstretched volley from the edge of the box to the top right-hand corner of the goal.

Having nearly had the Cup dashed from our hands, there was no way we would let it slip now. In the replay at Maine Road, I again watched from the sidelines as United found their form, with Andrei Kanchelskis being particularly lethal on the right.

Because of this replay, I missed one league game fewer and, by strange coincidence, that meant I would be available to play against my old club, Leeds, at Elland Road. Having just lost to Wimbledon beforehand, the game became another vital test for the side. The media decided to try to make it a personal grudge match between me and Howard Wilkinson and to raise the

8 May 1994: Manchester United celebrate their second Premiership title on the run. (Colorsport)

heat, but neither of us was interested in that. We wanted three points for our team, nothing more.

With the full squad at his disposal for the first time in many weeks, Alex Ferguson was later to say that our 2-0 win over Leeds was the best all-round performance he had seen from us all season. It certainly helped to silence the Leeds fans, who became fairly subdued, and meant that the press did not have the scenario they had predicted. Suddenly, the club felt transformed; the Double was back in sight.

Despite the valiant efforts of Kenny Dalglish's team to catch us, we were to repeat last year's form at the end of the season, finishing with a string of victories against Manchester City, Southampton and Ipswich. The final home game against Coventry was the moment for celebrating our second Premiership title on the run. In the end, the gods had smiled on us. Once we took the lead in the race, no one ever overtook us, even for a day. At the same time, we had managed to reach two cup finals.

We had played stylish football throughout the season, scoring 80 goals in the league – a tribute to our attacking play. In all games, I was to end as the leading scorer with 25 goals and my forward partner Mark Hughes managed 21 – both of us improving on last year's total and showing our growing understanding. What makes the side so dangerous, however, is that we are only two of the goalscorers – Ryan Giggs, Roy Keane, Paul Ince, Lee Sharpe and Andrei Kanchelskis all contributed several to the season's total. The threat from these players makes our job in attack easier, while we can hope to create chances for them.

I am proud that I belong to a side that is being compared with the great United teams of the past, and that we have honoured the names of Edwards, Charlton, Law, Best and the great Sir Matt Busby by trying to follow in their tradition. I am told that our 41 wins during the season in all competitions is three more than the record set in 1957 by the 'Busby Babes'. In losing only four league games, we had set another club record. All this, and we still have the FA Cup final to come – our 63rd game of the season (another record!). Having a week's break before the crowning event of the season, the final against Chelsea, was important for our spirits – especially as they were the only club to beat us twice, and the only club against whom we had not scored.

The English Cup final is unique, and I am not the only foreigner to have taken part who has watched it on television many times before actually playing in it. Both Andrei Kanchelskis and Peter Schmeichel were as aware as I was as to what this game means. For Chelsea, Dimitri Kharin and Erland Johnsen were both experiencing it for the first time, so the game was bound to have a continental flavour. It is a great occasion, made all the greater by the media build-up to it in the week before.

Cantona shoots his first penalty past goalkeeper Dimitri Kharin in United's 4-0 victory over Chelsea in the 1994 FA Cup final. (Colorsport)

Then came the match itself, with all the traditions, colour and excitement. In the first half, we do not play well and Chelsea hit the bar. Two penalties break the deadlock, and after that it could have been five or six goals as the spaces open up for us.

As I go to take the first penalty, the Chelsea captain Dennis Wise tries to disturb my concentration by betting me £100 that I will not score. Indeed, he had played for Wimbledon in their famous victory over Liverpool in 1988 when John Aldridge missed a penalty. But not this time. The Russian goalkeeper Kharin moves to his right at the last moment, but I see his move

Sharing a moment of triumph with Peter Schmeichel. In 1994 Manchester United became only the fourth team this century to win the Double. (Empics)

◀ *Holding the Premiership trophy, a familiar feeling.* (Colorsport)

and shoot to his left. For the first time this season against Chelsea, we are in front.

The second penalty is a replica of the first. Later, I am asked what I would have done if he had moved to the left. I answer that I would have shot to his right. As I explained earlier in this book, the penalty is easy to execute but the ultimate test to undertake. We are now in control, and Mark Hughes and Brian McClair, great servants to United, score to make it 4-0.

The Manchester United family celebrate the Double at a reception in the Metropole hotel. Isabelle, Raphaël and my brother Joël are at my side, while my father and Jean-Marie had been at the final – my blood family and my

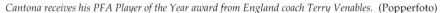

Cantona receives his PFA Player of the Year award from England coach Terry Venables. (Popperfoto)

football family all together. There are celebrations all night and photographs with the two trophies we have won.

The next morning a special train takes us back to Manchester for a tour of the city in an open-topped bus. It was a memorable occasion, with the supporters lining the road, decked out in rosettes and United jerseys, some with painted faces. Our route was ablaze with red and white banners and flags. The Double, about which you can only dream, had been achieved by Tottenham, Arsenal and Liverpool this century. Now we had matched their success.

To be a part of such a unique triumph for a club like Manchester United is a wonderful feeling. So it was to be chosen by my fellow professionals as the Player of the Year. I owe this honour to my colleagues at Old Trafford and to the role I have been allowed to play in the team. It suits me to have the freedom to create, invent and to drift unnoticed into positions from which I can make or score goals. I am grateful to Alex Ferguson and Brian Kidd for devising those tactics, and to all my team-mates who contribute so much to my own personal success. Not all managers allow their players such freedom to express themselves fully on the pitch, nor are they able to ensure that it fits the team plan at the same time.

I try to explain all of this in my speech at the PFA dinner – another unique English occasion which brings together all the game's stars, dressed up in dinner jackets. Where else could this happen?

Another proud moment for me this season was when the new manager of France, Aimé Jacquet, asked me to be the captain of the national team. It was a wonderful feeling when I led the side out to play in a friendly against Italy. Jacquet has kept many of the same players as before, but the tactics will be different. To wear the armband of captain is an honour which brings responsibilities. I am aware that I must serve as an example to the rest of the team, and I will do my best to ensure that France will again be at the forefront of world soccer.

It is a pity that we shall not be playing in the World Cup in the United States, but I hope that England will prove a happy hunting ground for me again in 1996 when France will, I pray, reach the finals of the European Championship. What a dream it would be to play at Old Trafford en route to the final at Wembley. I have a vision of France playing in England and bringing to the English supporters the sort of style, panache and magic which has been associated with many of United's games at Old Trafford.

I will be going to the World Cup as co-commentator for French television. It will be a new experience for me, and I am looking forward to it. I will be giving my own views on players, tactics and matches. Perhaps a current player can bring a different insight to the commentary. Whether or not it is something I will pursue after I retire from the game, at this stage I can only say that I look on it as a new challenge and a fresh opportunity. Indeed, I have always liked to have the impulse and stimulus which new activities can bring, so maybe there will be other new opportunities to try out in the future.

All that we have done at Manchester United is now history, a thing of the past. We must look forward and aspire to greater things. What would be greater than winning the European Cup next year? This last season, our early exit at the hands of Galatasaray was our biggest disappointment. We must not let that happen again. Watching AC Milan play against Barcelona in the European Cup final, we have seen the standards we must aim for. And we will. The club and the people of Manchester deserve that honour.

Chapter Eleven

·······································

A Voyage to Success

In Manchester, the first day of October 1995 was bright and crisp, with a light breeze. It was the perfect day for football, ideal for the big game being staged at Old Trafford that afternoon, the game which saw the return of Eric Cantona. The season was five weeks old and United had got off to an indifferent start.

They had occupied top spot in the Premiership for one Saturday night, dropping to second place the following day as Newcastle continued in formidable form. In the Coca-Cola Cup they had suffered a major setback losing 3-0 at home to York City in the first leg of their opening tie, but, perhaps more disappointingly, they were out of that season's European competition. Rotor Volgograd ended hopes of a run in the UEFA Cup by scoring twice at Old Trafford following a goalless first leg in Russia. United lost the 'away goals' rule, despite a sensational headed equaliser scored by goalkeeper Peter Schmeichel. His actions prevented the added embarrassment of seeing a 40-year record come to an end. United have never lost at home in a European competition, had Schmeichel not joined his outfield colleagues in the Russian penalty area to force home a cross they would most certainly have been beaten that night.

Of the seven league games played, United had won five, drawn one and lost once. Championship contenders Newcastle had won six, but had suffered a controversial defeat at Southampton and those were the only points they had dropped. United fans were satisfied with some of the early results. Alex Ferguson had changed the side significantly and things were ticking over as they waited for the big day.

At last, it arrived. Eric Cantona was about to step back into the game, and his return had been carefully stage-managed by television.

When the Premier League was launched in 1992 a deal was agreed with satellite television to allow the screening of live games. Under this, BSkyB were able to dictate the scheduling of matches so that they could be seen at peak viewing times. United had been due to face Liverpool on Saturday 30

Cantona's return was a major event for football – and TV. (Colorsport)

September. However, with Cantona's ban ending the following day, the piper once again called the tune and the game was moved on 24 hours. Perfect for television, perfect for football.

Almost up to the day of his return, there had been doubts about Eric's future. Despite assurances he would stay at Old Trafford, the predictions that he might walk out continued. Some critics said he would disappear before he was due to play again, others gave him days, weeks, perhaps at the most a few months before he would quit under the pressures.

As the day of his return approached, there were more suggestions that he would not be able to cope with the goading he was bound to receive from rival supporters. Columnists were divided in their opinion on whether or not he should have been allowed to remain in the game, but all agreed that he would face immense provocation. There would be a thousand Matthew Simmons at every away game, each ready to challenge the Frenchman and test his self-control.

It would be the same on the pitch. Ex-professionals said it was part of sport to use gamesmanship and to push opponents to their limit. Now that they had seen what a supporter had made Cantona do, some players would certainly try and force him to the brink. It was all speculation and, as it turned out, no one came close to predicting what would actually happen in the months that followed.

United had played 32 games since the incident at Selhurst Park and, without Eric's influence in the closing stages of the previous season, had seen success slip through their fingers. After losing the title by drawing the closing game at West Ham, manager Ferguson could not hide his disappointment. It was not that his players had performed badly that afternoon, but luck was not on their side, and the one vital goal they needed had eluded them. If they could have scrambled the ball home in those frantic dying minutes when the West Ham goal was under siege, they would have been champions for a third season in succession. It was not to be, but even so, Ferguson bravely faced the media within minutes of learning that Blackburn were champions.

'You get your money's worth watching us, that's for sure,' he said. 'It was breathtaking stuff, and we should have done it in the final minutes. We just needed a little bit of luck, that little break, the ball was hitting defenders, it was scrambled clear; it was really exciting stuff and I am really proud of the players – it has been a fantastic effort by them. They are gutted. You would expect them to be when you get as close as that. It was very disappointing for them. But they have handled adversity before and they will bounce back.'

No one dared to ask him if they would have done better with Eric Cantona in the side.

Stunned at losing the championship and by defeat in the FA Cup final, there were more shocks for United supporters during the summer of 1995. Paul Ince was sold to Inter Milan, who had also tried to persuade the club to let Eric move to Italy. Mark Hughes decided his days at Old Trafford were over and joined Chelsea, and as the new season began an unhappy Andrei Kanchelskis pulled himself free of a five-year contract and signed for Everton.

The exodus caused a sensation, with claims that Alex Ferguson was putting a noose around his own neck. Hughes and Ince went on the same day, with chairman Martin Edwards stating: 'If we were to lift a trophy next year, people would say that it was not so bad after all. If, however, things turn sour they will point to this particular issue as being the start of it.'

Some observers felt Edwards was covering himself against imminent disaster when he added that it was the manager who would 'stand or fall' by those transfer decisions. The buck it seemed would stop with Alex Ferguson.

Because of this, the most successful manager in the country suddenly found his judgement being questioned. There were the not unexpected comments from the tabloid press, but these caused few ripples. However, the actions of the local newspaper the *Manchester Evening News* did not simply stir the surface of what had been fairly calm waters, but created a tidal wave. Ferguson was deeply hurt. The paper asked its readers to phone in and vote on the issue: 'Should Fergie go?'

It was totally unexpected. The *Manchester Evening News* has a reputation for fair play. It never shirks its duty to report the truth and will criticise if and when necessary, but more often than not it comes down on the side of the club. It is regarded by supporters as one source of true information when sometimes the national press goes overboard. To stage such a stunt implied that there were reasons to believe that the club might be thinking of replacing the manager. All the telephone poll did was severely damage relationships between the manager and his local newspaper. The outcome of the voting – which was that Ferguson should remain in his job – was irrelevant. It was the action that Alex Ferguson will never forget, or forgive.

United fans showed their loyalty to the manager by chanting his name loud and long as they gathered for the pre-season friendlies. 'We are Fergie's red and white army!' they proclaimed, and greeted him with rapturous applause. He has always had a great rapport with the supporters and he knew he could rely on them. They did not need to phone a newspaper to pledge their support. Ferguson was the man who had brought success back to the club. He had built the team which ended the long wait for the Championship. He had gone further even than Sir Matt Busby by winning the Double. He had also given them Eric Cantona.

'I think we have listened to a lot of diatribe in the summer and I have absolutely no feeling of having let anyone down and the support must know that about me. That is the last thing I would want,' Ferguson said before getting down to business as the season began. 'I have made one decision which I felt was in the interests of Manchester United and that is what I will always do. Alex Ferguson is not important, it is the supporters and the club that is important.' That decision was to part with Ince; Hughes and Kanchelskis went of their own accord.

In an attempt to strengthen his squad and replace Kanchelskis, the manager made a bid for Tottenham and England winger Darren Anderton but was rejected. It meant that United would go into the new campaign without any new faces in the side, without three key players and with Eric Cantona still weeks away from a comeback.

In the first game at Aston Villa it was obvious from the start that the influence of Ince was missing. Without the strength of Hughes, the speed of Kanchelskis, and the guile of Cantona, United looked vulnerable. It was

In beating Chelsea 3–0 on 17 April 1993 Manchester United were well on their way to their first league title in 26 years. Cantona scored United's third goal in the 48th minute. (*Empics*)

Handshakes all round after a game of head tennis with fellow French international Laurent Blanc while on holiday in Djerba, Tunisia, in June 1993.

May 1994: Cantona takes his turn to lift the Premiership trophy. (*Popperfoto*)

Cantona scores his second goal from the penalty spot in the 1994 FA Cup final against Chelsea. (*Popperfoto*)

The Manchester United team celebrate their Double triumph. (*Colorsport*)

Manager Alex Ferguson congratulates Cantona following United's 2–0 win over rivals Blackburn Rovers in the 1994 Charity Shield. (*Popperfoto*)

The focus of attention as a group of Japanese tourists arrives on the beach at Djerba, June 1993.

Cantona describes his relationship with Manchester United as 'a love story'. Here he shows his feelings after scoring against Blackburn Rovers on 22 January 1995. (*Colorsport*)

Welcome back! Liverpool's Ian Rush shakes Cantona's hand as the teams draw 2–2 in the Frenchman's first match following his eight-month ban. (*Colorsport*)

4 March 1996: the crunch encounter with league leaders Newcastle United at St James' Park. Cantona scores the only goal of the game to pull Manchester United to within one point of their rivals. (*Empics*)

Manchester United collect the Premiership trophy at Middlesbrough on 5 May to become champions for three out of the last four seasons. (*Colorsport*)

FA Cup-winners 1996: Manchester United celebrate their historic double Double. (*Empics*)

The end? The last game of the 1996-97 season and a tired-looking Cantona pulls on John Moncur's shirt after United's 2-0 victory over West Ham. Exactly a week later football was stunned by the news of King Eric's decision to retire from the game. (*Mark Leech*)

perhaps no surprise that Villa led 3-0 by the interval, but immediately the knives were out. Headlines were being prepared well before the final whistle, and losing 3-1 was not the best way to prove to the critics that United could cope after the summer's activities.

'Forget it!' said one tabloid. There would be no success for United this season. 'You will never win anything with kids,' television pundit Alan Hansen declared. Like the *Manchester Evening News* poll, those words would not be forgotten.

Ferguson felt he could win something with his young players, or at least he could give them the chance to prove themselves at the top level and replaced his missing stars with youngsters from the 1992 youth team. He was prepared to face the consequences as David Beckham, Nicky Butt, brothers Gary and Philip Neville, Paul Scholes, Simon Davies and John O'Kane were all included in the squad for the opening game. Beckham scored the consolation goal after the manager changed the pattern of play for the second half and he was comforted by the fact that they showed some confidence despite the disappointment of the first spell.

Victories over West Ham and Wimbledon at Old Trafford, followed by a creditable 2-1 win at Ewood Park against champions Blackburn boosted morale, as well as the hopes of the faithful. Then they went to Goodison Park and beat Everton 3-2 in a game in which Andrei Kanchelskis faced his former club for the first time. It ended disastrously for the Ukrainian who fell awkwardly and dislocated a shoulder following a challenge by Lee Sharpe during the first quarter of an hour. He was out of action for several weeks. In the final Premiership games without Cantona, they drew 0-0 with Sheffield Wednesday at Hillsborough and beat newly promoted Bolton 3-0 at Old Trafford.

Football held its breath. It was time for King Cantona to parade before his loyal subjects once again. Eric had prepared for his return for several weeks. He had remained in training since the day of his suspension, keeping himself fit but unable to play in competitive games. Alex Ferguson stepped up his schedule by arranging a series of friendly matches against local sides, but it was one of these which led to more problems for Cantona.

News leaked that Eric was playing in a friendly match at The Cliff, the club's training ground. Unknown to United, a photographer gained access and took pictures of the Frenchman in action. It all seemed fairly innocent until these were published, then the Football Association stepped in. They were indignant that their ban had been breached. They reiterated that the suspension was 'from all footballing activities' and this included such practice matches. They viewed Eric's inclusion in the friendly games as a breach of the suspension and, although the club did not think that they had done anything wrong, they found themselves in hot water.

It was bureaucracy at its best. United protested, pointing out that there was little difference to Cantona facing eleven players from Rochdale or Bury to taking part in a first XI versus reserve XI game. The FA relented and Eric was allowed to play on, yet the intervention of the FA came very close to driving him out, frustrated and deeply upset by the attitude of those at Lancaster Gate. He had every right to feel this way. He had served the civil sentence imposed for the offence he had committed, had completed the ban imposed by his club, and was close to the end of the additional period added by the disciplinary tribunal. Even a murderer could expect some remission for good behaviour.

So the games were allowed to continue on the proviso that the public was not admitted, but efforts to prevent supporters from watching them failed. Hundreds gathered on the river bank beyond the boundaries of the training ground, peering through the wire mesh and cheering their hero. Had matters been left as they were, the club would simply have closed the doors of the training ground at the appropriate time and got on with the games. Because of the added publicity, hundreds more turned up causing traffic chaos and security problems.

Getting pictures of Cantona in action now became big business and the media seagulls went to great lengths to photograph the French star. Ladders appeared against the training ground wall, with cameramen peering over to get a shot of him walking to or from his car. Money was offered for access to bedroom windows, back yards and balconies of houses overlooking The Cliff and the whole thing reached quite ridiculous proportions. Throughout it all Eric remained calm, quietly going about his job and refusing to be riled by increasing attention. He refused to speak to radio, television and newspapers apart from passing the time of day with those of us who saw him regularly. Requests were met with a polite, 'Perhaps I will speak one day, but not today…'

Eric is a warm, friendly man with a sharp sense of humour but is wary of who he can trust when it comes to his contact with the media. He would share a joke with the regulars, yet still would not be drawn into a conversation which could find its way into print.

He has, however, always found time for the supporters. He will go out of his way to mix with them and, despite their increasing numbers at training sessions, will find the time to sign autographs no matter how many demands are made, pose for photographs and shake countless hands. It is a genuine show of affection rather than any form of public relations and one which would surprise any of his critics who think that Cantona is aloof, arrogant or out of reach.

I have never seen him refuse to sign an autograph, or refuse to have his photograph taken by his fans. He will pose rather sheepishly, holding a baby, with his arm around a teenage supporter or bending down to be close to a child in a wheelchair. He will walk along the lines of fans leaning on the crush barriers which cordon off part of the training ground car park, signing and chatting, then when he has finished go back again to see if anyone has missed out. By now the whole population of Manchester should have Eric's autograph!

Four days before his comeback, United decided to call a truce on those they were preventing from getting close to their star. They wanted to put an end to the ladders, the snatched pictures, and the cloak-and-dagger efforts to beat their security. The doors to Old Trafford were opened to the media, with photographers and television crews invited to watch the players train.

Once the session had finished Alex Ferguson made himself available for a press conference, but we were told that Eric would not be appearing. As soon as he had finished training, he disappeared into the dressing room with the rest of his colleagues while manager Ferguson addressed the gathering crammed into the club's interview theatre.

Ferguson:
I felt an open day like this would get the thing out of the road, then we can get down to preparing for Sunday's game which is an important one for us. If I can trust you, and rely on you to leave us alone now I would be grateful. I am not surprised at all the interest. I suppose it was inevitable, it is something we just have to get on with.

Had Cantona changed?

Ferguson:
I have noticed this week that he has been quite quiet, quieter than normal, and obviously there will be some mental preparation going on. I think that is the only change. We hope that he has learned his lesson. I would not think that anyone would want to go down that road again. I don't think anyone will ever get that kind of ban again particularly in England, and I don't think he would want to suffer all that, for himself, for his family.

It must have been very difficult, but he has not said anything about it. He took his punishment, accepted the community service and did very well at that. He has trained really hard, I think he has only missed one session since pre-season and what he needs now is football. In terms of the game, he has not done a lot wrong on the field. There have been excesses, and obviously the last incident was something we could never anticipate.

He defended the decision to give Cantona another chance.

Ferguson:
There are very few players in the modern game who are true Manchester United players, who can live up to the expectations of our supporters, the type of player they have been used to for decades. Ability is more to do with it than anything else. He is no problem to us. In training he is magnificent, his dedication and preparation as a footballer is first class. I think there may be times when he will lose his temper again during a game, but there are plenty of players who do that. He has to live with the fact of who he is, but he also knows he has got to show maturity and responsibility.

What I did was make a decision which suited Manchester United in terms of his ability as a footballer, and I am absolutely certain that I have done the right thing. If he goes back to his form of his first year with us, then we are going to be a much better team.

He said that the club was worried that Cantona would become a target. They would overcome the 'fastest-gun' syndrome by stepping up security especially at away games. Ned Kelly, whose company was responsible for much of the ground control at Old Trafford, would handle this. He quickly earned himself the tag of being Eric's 'minder'.

Ferguson:
It is out on the football field that we are more concerned about. I know that supporters will boo every time he gets the ball but that is not a problem for Eric.

No one could predict what lay ahead, but Ferguson said that he was confident that Cantona would handle all the problems which he might face. He said that he did not think the striker would quit if the harassment became too much for him, but he also realised that they were sailing into uncharted waters.

Ferguson:
I have a reasonable amount of confidence that he will stay. He wants to play here. He has shown his most consistent form as a footballer here, he has a support that idolises him, he is happy being with the club and

it is a good club to play for. There are a lot of advantages for us. There are a lot of things for Eric to consider if he ever thought about wanting to move. There are a lot of plusses for us. There is bound to be a bit of apprehension for the lad because he hasn't played for nine months.

The media won't have any sympathy for him. When you come to do your match report on Sunday that won't come into it. It will be how he has performed. It is a big game for Eric. I think the adrenaline will help him, but what we will face is that after about three or four games a flatness will come into it. Having been out for so long there will come two or three games where it will go a little bit flat before he can take off again.

I have no fears for Sunday, I think he will last the game. He will be tired and will probably take little rests during the game, but I think he will last it. What he will offer is his ability to be in space to open up the defence, his composure on the ball, his assurance. Those things don't vanish, he will always have that.

We did extremely well to get where we got last season without Eric, taking it right to the wire in the league. I don't think we had any right to think we could have got there with the one or two injuries we had, the suspensions, the media attention which turned on the club. We came through that really well and it says a lot for the character of the people in here that they managed to get as close as they did.

In some ways we have overcome the Eric Cantona syndrome, but, like Bryan Robson before him, you want him in your side because players like that do have a special influence on the team. Even in his last days, Bryan always had an influence when he was on the field and Eric will have an influence. All we want is for him to be treated the same as anyone else.

Building work on the giant new North Stand meant that Old Trafford's capacity was reduced to just below 35,000 for the big game. Before the season began, United had announced that during the construction of the three-tier grandstand which would hold 26,500, and swell attendances to more than 55,000, no visiting supporters would be admitted. It was a temporary measure, but the crowd was totally partisan as Eric stepped out into the sunlight.

He was greeted with rapturous applause, and, as kick-off approached, the crowd was in full voice singing its own version of 'The Marseillaise' and the carol 'The Twelve Days of Christmas'. Whoever created the latter used little imagination but plenty of humour. 'On the first day of Christmas my true love gave to me, an Eric Cantona. On the second day of Christmas my true

love gave to me two Eric Cantonas and an Eric Cantona.' And
so it goes on.

The crowd got its early Christmas present that day. The King
was back. Eric's return had
sparked off a rush of trade at
United's Mega-Store, the giant
souvenir shop at the rear of the
stadium. Cantona shirts were in
big demand with more number
sevens sold than any other.

One supporter is reported to
have asked not for the name
'Cantona' but for 'God' to be
added to the back of his shirt. He
was told that the club did not like
to do this on religious grounds,

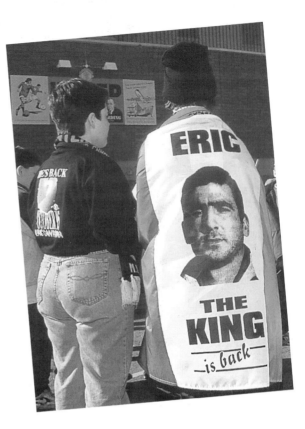

The fans 'never stopped to sing my name'.
(Colorsport)

1 October 1995: business as usual for Cantona in his first match after his ban. (Colorsport)

but was made an offer he could not refuse: 'You can have Cantona for the same price as God!' There is little you can say about that!

The teams emerged for kick-off and the crowd exploded. The moment they had all waited for had at last arrived. There he was with that familiar straight-backed walk which gave him that seeming air of arrogance. It was the same as it had been the day he first stepped out at Old Trafford for the second half of a derby game against City. The flicks, the vision, the back heels, the skills were all still there. He was an immediate success.

United could not have got off to a better start. In the first minute they took the lead with Eric creating the goal with virtually his first touch. Nicky Butt forced the ball home from close range, but King Cantona really was back and the crowd sensed that success was in the air again.

It would not come that particular afternoon though. Liverpool fought hard. They were the form team and showed it when Robbie Fowler levelled the scores after 33 minutes, then silenced the home fans with a chip over

Schmeichel's head 20 minutes later. For 17 minutes the visitors led. Then Ryan Giggs burst through but was pulled back by his shirt by Rob Jones. Referee David Elleray pointed to the spot and Old Trafford erupted again. It was a penalty, and the moment of truth had come.

Eric picked up the ball and stepped forward. He placed it on the spot, turned away from goal then took two strides forwards and rammed his shot to the left of David James as the keeper moved in the opposite direction. The crowd went wild with delight and they were not alone. Chased by his team-mates Eric ran behind the goal, and leaped at a net support swinging round

Wild jubilation following Cantona's spot-kick goal in United's 2-2 draw with arch rivals Liverpool. The King was back. (Empics)

on it like a fireman descending on a slippery pole. Then he jumped over the advertising hoardings and into the crowd to embrace them. It was total elation, Old Trafford was a sea of leaping happy people and Eric Cantona was the happiest of them all. What a contrast with the last time he had taken a leap towards a spectator.

The game ended in a 2-2 draw, and United stayed in third place behind Newcastle and Aston Villa.

Two days later United had to play York City in the return leg of their Coca-Cola Cup tie. The game at Bootham Crescent would see Eric closer to supporters than he would be at many Premiership grounds, and with United under pressure as they trailed 0-3 from the first game there were predictions that Cantona could have problems. The game went without a hitch, the home fans were sporting and did little to rile anyone. United won 3-1 but bowed out thanks to York's supremacy at Old Trafford. The York fans were too happy to think about causing problems for Eric Cantona.

Then came a blow. To build up his match fitness, Alex Ferguson decided that Eric should play in a reserve game at Old Trafford the following Saturday. It attracted a remarkable crowd of 21,502, most of them parents with young children taking advantage of much reduced prices to see Eric Cantona in action.

They were disappointed. Within 18 minutes, Eric limped off after taking a kick on the knee from Leeds midfielder Jason Blunt. The cynics claimed that there had been no intentions of him playing the whole 90 minutes, and that the game had been used as a money-making ploy by the club. Such is life for Manchester United, but not only were such suggestions ridiculous they were far from the truth.

The injury was serious enough to rule Eric out of the next Premiership game against Manchester City, yet despite his absence United won 1-0. So came Chelsea at Stamford Bridge, the first real test on territory which is far from friendly as far as United are concerned. It was an encounter with a plot full of many twists. Mark Hughes would be facing his former club; for Eric it was the vociferous Chelsea fans on his return to London for the first time since the January fixture at Crystal Palace. To add more interest, the man in charge that afternoon was none other than Alan Wilkie, the referee who had sent Eric from the field at Selhurst Park.

The fans were hostile, but no more than they usually are for a United visit. There were three bookings, and Chelsea's Frank Sinclair was sent off two minutes from time, but not once did Eric step out of line.

It was something we would get used to as the season progressed, Eric Cantona calmly going about his business not getting involved, acting as the peacemaker if trouble flared. His brief from manager Ferguson following his return was that he should not make challenges which could lead to retaliatory situations. Tackling is not one of Eric's strongest points.

At Chelsea he played in his familiar position behind the front runners, directing operations and, with Paul Scholes outstanding, United won 4-1.

In the months which followed, provocation from rival spectators was ignored by Eric and attempts to rile him on the field became fewer when opponents realised that he was not going to react. However, his presence and influence helped transform the side once again. This was the new improved Cantona, a changed character who walked away from controversy.

In the Premiership, the gap between United and leaders Newcastle widened as winter set in. Two points separated the sides after United beat Bryan Robson's Middlesbrough at Old Trafford, but the difference grew to five following defeat at Arsenal.

December was a disaster. It began with a 1-1 draw in the return game against Chelsea in which Eric was booked for a foul, his only caution of the entire season. The squad was depleted by injuries and suspensions, with

By winter 1995 Newcastle United were in a commanding lead in the Premiership and December began badly for Manchester United with a 1-1 draw against Chelsea. (Empics)

The crowd give Eric a helping hand but the team's form has slumped. It looks unlikely that Newcastle can be caught. (Empics)

Peter Schmeichel out after having an operation on his elbow, and Gary Pallister sidelined after injuring his back. Roy Keane had been sent off against Middlesbrough, his second dismissal of the season following a harsh red card at Blackburn, and served his suspension as he recovered from a hernia operation, this too was his second of the year. Nicky Butt accumulated 21 disciplinary points and was given a three-match ban, and to add to this Steve Bruce picked up a hamstring injury. It was no surprise when form slumped.

It seemed there was little hope of winning the championship; Newcastle were in the driving seat, swept along by a run of victories and their enthusiastic support. Eric scored twice in the home game with Sheffield Wednesday, his first goals since the day of his return, but the game was the third successive draw and was followed by defeats at Leeds and Liverpool.

Newcastle's lead had increased by ten points and Ferguson searched for a defender to bridge the gap left by Pallister's absence. He turned to Frenchman William Prunier, a friend of Eric's and a free agent. He came on trial, and watched from the grandstand in what many felt was the game of

Cantona scores twice against Sheffield Wednesday at Old Trafford but Manchester United can only manage a draw. (Empics)

the season so far, their first clash with Newcastle. United outplayed their rivals to improve their hopes of making a challenge. Keane gave a superb performance in the 2-0 win and, three days later, Prunier made his debut against QPR. United won 2-1 with the trialist doing enough to be included in the side for the New Year's day game at Tottenham.

It was the last we saw of Prunier, who made a swift return to his homeland following a 4-1 defeat, the heaviest United had endured since the Premiership was launched. Ferguson asked him to stay longer, but unlike Eric Cantona, English football was not for him.

Those early-season predictions seemed to have a ring of truth about them, were United destined to fail for a second successive year? The defeat at Tottenham could have been seen by many as the end; it was, however, the beginning.

Inspired by a burst of goals from Cantona, United went on a run which started with the somewhat fortunate 2-2 home draw against Sunderland in the third round of the FA Cup, when Eric's equaliser kept them in the

3 February 1996: Cantona's first appearance at Selhurst Park since the incident that led to his eight-month ban. (Colorsport)

The visit is much-hyped: he answers his critics by scoring two goals in the encounter with Wimbledon. (Empics)

competition. A draw with Aston Villa was followed by ten consecutive wins. Cantona was in explosive form, scoring the only goal at West Ham, two against Wimbledon on his media-hyped return to Selhurst Park, and Cup goals against Reading in the fourth round, a penalty against Manchester City in the fifth round, which levelled the scores before Lee Sharpe struck the winner.

United were through to the quarter-finals of the Cup, and in second place in the Premiership though still nine points adrift of Newcastle. The Tynesiders were clear favourites, but there were signs that the pressure was getting to them and their form started to slip.

Eric had chalked up ten goals since his return, seven in the league, three in the Cup. Four had come from penalties, and he had hauled himself to within one goal of leading scorer Paul Scholes even though he had played only four months of the season. During the period Eric was suspended, Denis Irwin had taken on the responsibility of penalty kicks, scoring twice. When Eric converted that first spot kick against Liverpool in his comeback game he helped maintain a 100 per cent record going back to February 1993, the last time United had missed a penalty.

Ironically Cantona was not one of the scorers in the game which turned out to be United's biggest victory of the season, and which helped pave the way for the success which was to follow.

They were away to neighbours and long-time rivals Bolton Wanderers, who were fighting to survive in the Premiership. Within four minutes Bolton almost scored, but United survived and then the rout started. By the end of the afternoon the 6-0 scoreline said it all. The heat was on Newcastle and the two were destined to meet in the next game as now only four points separated the sides.

There was an injury scare before the confrontation. Eric was under treatment for a calf injury which had seen him cutting short his appearance in the Bolton game. He trotted off after 73 minutes and spent the early part of the following week on the treatment table. He responded well and was able to face Newcastle.

For the first time, United really found themselves on hostile territory. Support for the home side was fanatical and although anti-Cantona activity had reduced drastically in the months following his return, it peaked that night.

In the past there had been the expected chanting, booing and cat-calls, but when supporters discovered that it was having no effect they had got on with encouraging their own side. Not so at Newcastle, where David Ginola, a colleague of Cantona's in the French national side, was one of their players. He had made it clear in newspaper articles and interviews that he and Cantona did not see eye to eye and that set the scene for the next drama of the season.

United were goaded as they alighted from the team coach, jeered as they warmed up and in the game itself, forced back by Newcastle for the first 45 minutes. Peter Schmeichel was in remarkable form making save after save and his defence stood solid around him. At one point he was beaten by a goalbound shot, but it was headed away from the line by none other than Eric Cantona! It seemed to be just a matter of time before Newcastle would take the lead. Could United stand the onslaught? One man had the answer. Eric Cantona.

The second half was a transformation. United came more and more into the game, having soaked up all the home side could offer. Ginola was booked for a foul born of frustration and it was time for Eric to take command. Fifty-one minutes had gone, Andy Cole forced the ball out to Philip Neville on the left flank and the young full back ran forward a few yards, crossed, and Eric met the ball on the right-hand edge of the penalty area. He took it in his stride and hit a low half-volley which bounced beyond the reach of Srnicek in the Newcastle goal. Again the taunters had been silenced.

The gap at the top was one point and now United knew that they could do it. The Premiership title was within reach and the task which had seemed impossible at Christmas became a probability by Easter.

The goal at Newcastle sparked off another scoring run from Cantona. A week later he got the first against Southampton as United reached the semi-final of the FA Cup, but it was in the next Premiership fixture that he scored what could have been one of the most crucial goals of the season. It was at Loftus Road, and Queens Park Rangers led 2-1 with minutes to go. Unfortunately, the stadium clock had broken down with around twenty minutes of the game remaining and there was confusion among the home fans. They know that when its screen is blank, 90 minutes are up. Whistling began after 80 minutes as the fans tried to encourage the referee to blow for time. Referee Hart added stoppage time as the restlessness increased and when Eric scored halfway through the four minutes he allowed there was an almighty row.

The point United earned from the draw was of immense value to them, but the two lost by Rangers contributed to their eventual relegation. Steve Bruce made the goal, battling to win the ball in the QPR penalty area, and his pass to Giggs was crossed to Eric at the far post. From a position similar to where he had got his goal at Newcastle, Cantona scored and United went top of the Premiership for the first time since their short stay in September.

Again, within 48 hours, Newcastle overtook them, but two more Cantona goals tilted the see-saw back in United's favour. The first of these came against Arsenal at Old Trafford where he fired home a brilliant dipping volley of such ferocity that David Seaman would have risked a limb had he tried to stop it. Tottenham were next and this time Eric's winner went between a defender's legs. Power one day, subtlety the next.

Eric had scored nine goals in twelve games and United were top of the Premiership, although Newcastle had two games in hand. Throughout all this, Eric still remained silent. Requests for interviews were politely refused but the Cantona wit showed through.

Eric Bilderman, a French journalist from *L'Equipe* magazine, arrived at the training ground with a gift of some fine wines brought over from France. The two chatted for a while then M. Cantona went to his car, put the wine in his boot thanking M. Bilderman for his generosity. 'He said "thank you", took the wine but still would not give me the interview!' said the bewildered sports-writer, as Eric drove away.

Although he had never confided in any of the local journalists who he saw regularly, we formed the opinion that he would break his vow of silence once United had won something. We were sure that Eric felt guilty because he had let his colleagues down that night at Selhurst Park, he wanted none of the limelight until matters had been corrected.

There was a distinct possibility that United would end the season successfully. Apart from their efforts to overtake Newcastle, they reached the FA Cup final by beating Chelsea 2-1 at Villa Park in a semi-final once again hyped up by the media because it brought together Mark Hughes and Manchester United once more.

By Easter Monday, United had turned that ten-point Christmas deficit into a six-point lead over Newcastle. The impossible seemed possible, with two more Cantona goals helping United earn maximum points. He scored the first from a penalty at Maine Road where City were beaten 3-2 on Easter Saturday, then got the only goal of the afternoon as struggling Coventry lost at Old Trafford. It was his 17th of the season, his 13th in the Premiership and he was now leading scorer, an illustration of his determination to bring back success to the club.

But there had been more to Eric's return to football than his ability to score important goals. He was a changed character in the eyes of many. He had been booked just that once and when Steve Bruce was injured he had been given the captaincy of the side by Alex Ferguson, leading his young comrades by example. His behaviour was impeccable and it was to earn him praise from all quarters, including the Football Writers' Association. The week before United beat Nottingham Forest 5-0 and Eric scored his final league goal of the season, he had been voted Footballer of the Year. It was another amazing turn around, the very seagulls who had followed in his wake a year earlier, were now to honour him.

The election of the writers' top player is carried out in the weeks preceding the FA Cup final. All members of the FWA, journalists who earn their living by reporting on the game, are entitled to vote. The inevitable lobbying follows and it is rare that speculation about who has won turns out to be wrong. When Eric's name emerged from those in contention there were a few raised eyebrows. The new, improved Cantona had no doubt convinced the voters that he was a suitable choice, but the more cynical saw the award as at least one way of getting a story out of the Frenchman.

The Footballer of the Year always makes a speech of acceptance and here was the perfect ploy, how could someone awarded what is considered by

Cantona helps United to a convincing 5-0 win over Nottingham Forest and a thrilling climax to the season. (Colorsport)

many to be a top honour snub his hosts by refusing to speak? If it was a ploy it worked, and eventually he did make his speech. However, the award was more than likely a genuine gesture on behalf of many of those who realised that there was more to Eric Cantona than the blemishes on the surface they had seen a year before.

He really was a highly polished performer now fully restored to all his glory.

On the Sunday after defeating Forest, United were away to Middlesbrough in the closing league game of the season. At the same time Newcastle were at home to Tottenham Hotspur. During the week leading up to the game, Newcastle had drawn at Nottingham Forest and used up their games in hand. To prevent United from winning the Championship Newcastle had to beat Tottenham at St James' Park, while United lost to Bryan Robson's new club.

There was little chance of that happening, although Middlesbrough started in lively enough fashion to scare the champions elect. Steve Bruce was out of the side because of a hamstring injury and, with Eric as captain, United won 3-0.

It was a great achievement for a side which had been given little chance at the start of the season, and yet there was even more success to come. The Championship cheers had hardly died down as preparations for the following Saturday's FA Cup final moved into full swing. United held a media day from which Eric was absent and it became apparent that as part of the television deal with the BBC for coverage of the game, United had agreed to him being interviewed.

His speech at the FWA dinner had made little impact. It was polite, humorous and misunderstood when he referred to 'critics', instead of using the word 'criticism', saying that while he had taken notice of some, others 'were fit for only one place. The toilet!'

So on Saturday 11 May, as United prepared to face Liverpool in the annual battle for the FA Cup, Eric's interview with the BBC *Grandstand* presenter Desmond Lynam was broadcast to the millions waiting for the start of the big game. Viewers saw the true Eric Cantona for the first time. He appeared as a relaxed man willing to answer all of Lynam's questions. He lounged on a large settee, looked comfortable if slightly embarrassed and spoke in a soft sincere voice. At times his eyes welled as if he was close to tears as he spoke, at other times they sparked with a hint of mischief.

Cantona:
Winning the first Championship with Manchester United was great; this one is very important for the club after last season, and very important for myself. I had a lot of things to prove this season after the incident that everybody knows about last year. There was a lot of criticism but the critics can be very positive. I think that we learn from everything and a bad thing can be turned into a good thing. It is very difficult at the time, but if we think about the future we can use it to make the future brighter.

Alex Ferguson asked me if I wanted to leave English football, because he knew it was a very difficult time for me, and I just said 'No'! He did not try to persuade me because he knew it was a difficult time. He wanted me to stay, but only if I wanted to stay. I was close to signing for somebody else because I did not know if Manchester United wanted me to stay. I received a lot of criticism and so did the club, but I just wanted to stay.

Cantona was asked if Michel Platini had been the person who had first encouraged him to come to England.

Cantona:
When he came to speak to me I had stopped playing football. I had stopped for two months. I had quit the game and did not want to play any more, in France, Italy, Spain but he said that I must come back. I was 25 at the time and I said, 'No, I don't want to.' He suggested that I try England, but I said that it was very difficult for a foreigner to play in England because even though I had perhaps played 25 times for France at that time I was sure that they did not know me. But I got the chance; Leeds gave me the chance.

   When I first went to Manchester United I did not expect to do as well as I did. When I arrived there I felt that I was now in a big club, all the players around me were good and great. I knew that I had everything to prove but I wasn't afraid, I am very confident. I have always been like that. I am sorry but I am not arrogant like people say, I am just confident about myself.

Eric turned his attention to the English game and said that those who criticised it for its lack of skill and technique were wrong.

Cantona:
What is technique? For me it is pass, control, pass, the ability to score goals, the ability to tackle properly and for me the English players are the best. But if you speak about entertainment, creativity maybe they have to work more, but in terms of technique I think that the English players have got everything.

   I don't know if I influence the other players at Manchester United; I just work on what I feel I need to. If I don't score goals, if I miss chances I would stay fifteen minutes after training in front of a goalkeeper, ask somebody to cross the ball to me and try to score. If I was not happy with myself I would want to improve it.

   I think we will play [in the final] with more freedom now that we have won the Championship. I think last season we lost in the final because we did not win the league the week before. I was not playing, but it was my team-mates. It is like a big family.

Asked about the departure of Hughes, Ince and Kanchelskis, Eric said it had not affected him, although he admitted that they were his close friends.

Cantona:

I am too optimistic, I think that I can win a game if I play on my own against eleven players! I am not worried about anything, but I respected them and I still respect them because we had a lot of great times together. But life is like that, before us there was life, after us there will be another one. The young players who have come in have been wonderful, but the most important season for them is next season. After your first season you win the Championship you maybe think 'that's it', but next season will be the most difficult in their heads, but they will handle it.

With the Cup final only a few hours away there was strong speculation that Alex Ferguson would not risk regular skipper Steve Bruce. He had been having treatment for the injury which kept him out of the Championship-clinching game at Middlesbrough. If Bruce did not play at Wembley, Eric would be captain. Lynam asked him about his communication with the other players, he was not the type of leader who screamed instructions as some skippers did. How did he do it?

Cantona:

Maybe sometimes I want to say something, but I cannot find the word, and I don't have time to find the word. In football you have to think very quickly.

There was still strong speculation that Eric would be included in the French squad for the forthcoming European Championships, even though Aimé Jacquet, the national team manager, had overlooked both Cantona and David Ginola for his qualifying games. Did Eric want to play in the tournament?

Cantona:

I need a holiday, everybody needs a holiday after the long season in England. We have got the Champions League next season and the people who play in the European Championships will be tired like they were after the World Cup. It is always like that. AC Milan were not champions and Barcelona were not champions, Manchester United too, after the World Cup. It is very difficult and after the European Championships it will be the same.

As things turned out, Jacquet went into Euro 96 without Cantona and Ginola and the French reached the semi-finals. Before the game Jacquet said: 'I have no regrets about leaving Cantona out of the side. I am still friends with him and I think he is one of the best players in Europe, but we have done well without him and we can continue to succeed without him.'

They lost to the Czech Republic at Old Trafford, in a game which cried out for the skills and finishing touch of an Eric Cantona. So what lies ahead for the rejected star?

Cantona:
I think the next very important target for Manchester United will be the Champions League next season. We all want to win it. It is important for English football, for us, for everybody. If we don't win it the people will forget us. If you just win in your country you have no credibility. I think that all the players who do not play in the European Championships will have an advantage, but if I play I will be happy. If I don't play, I will go on holiday and I will be fit next season.

Eric revealed a remarkable philosophy as far as his approach to the game was concerned. He was asked what lay ahead in his career, and his thoughts about what he might do when he eventually stops playing.

Cantona:
When we win I want to stay in football, when we lose I want to quit! I don't know, perhaps one day I may be a manager or something here in England. We will stay here. I will stay for my children, because now they are at school here, they have got all their friends here, and they are very happy here and we are too.

He said that those who felt that the Selhurst Park incident had changed his life were incorrect.

Cantona:
I just do what I enjoy doing now. I try to live in harmony with myself and maybe that is to do with the way I play. Before it was something else and maybe in the future there will be something more. I just try, try to be in harmony with my body, with my mind and at the moment that is one.

He was asked about his feelings towards the Manchester United supporters and took us back to that moment when he had told me of his love affair with the club and those who followed it.

Cantona:
What can I say? I respect them very much, I love them but last season for

eight months they never stopped to sing my name, even if it was just for fifteen seconds in a game, they thought about it. I will never forget it, and I will try to give them the pleasure they need to receive for two more years – maybe longer, or maybe shorter – we never know in life. But I am very, very, very happy.

Eric Cantona won the hearts of many people through his television appearance that afternoon. Those who had been led to believe that he was some kind of two-headed monster because of what they had read or heard about the Manchester United star, were surprised to see someone who could openly speak about the love of his family, and how important it was to him. This was no villain, no thug, no ignoramus.

So to the final, and Alex Ferguson not for the first time found himself ripped apart by emotions as he named his side. His heart wanted him to include Steve Bruce, his head told him that he could not risk a player who was not fully fit. David May played in Bruce's place, Eric Cantona was captain.

It was a similar story in 1994 when Ferguson had left out Bryan Robson as

In the absence of Steve Bruce, Cantona was captain for the 1996 FA Cup final. (Popperfoto)

167

The double Double! The end of play and United team-mates congratulate Cantona, scorer of the only goal in the 1996 FA Cup final. Dejected Liverpool players cannot bear to look. (Colorsport)

United beat Chelsea to complete the Double. He had also found himself torn between loyalty to a player he regarded as a friend, and his quest for success when in 1990, goalkeeper Jim Leighton was dropped for the replayed final against Crystal Palace. A manager's life would never be an easy one.

The television audience saw the Cup final as a dull game, yet for many of those at Wembley it was a tense occasion as United created a unique niche for themselves in the history of the game. Fear of one another's attacking skills led to both sides using stifling tactics in midfield. United had the edge throughout but if ever a game cried out for a goal it was this one. Alex Ferguson must have been impressed by the way that his young players adapted to the tension of a Wembley final, but it was experience and not youth which won the game. The experience of Eric Cantona.

With extra time four minutes away, United won a corner on the right. As the cross came over David James, the Liverpool keeper, who all afternoon had handled the ball well, for once mis-judged his jump. He collided with one of his team-mates and could only palm the ball out of the penalty area. It ran to Eric who, leaning back to get into the correct position, his a powerful right foot volley through the ruck of players between him and goal. Wembley erupted, and that was that.

There was no way back for Liverpool who had lost direction well before that decisive strike. United's supporters celebrated, but the tension was electrifying for the last three minutes, and there was relief as Dermot Gallagher blew the final whistle.

United had won the double Double. Taking the league and FA Cup in the same season was an achievement in itself, to do it for a second time within the space of three seasons was incredible. No club in the history of English football had done it before them.

The players embraced in the centre of the pitch, Alex Ferguson and his assistant Brian Kidd ran out to congratulate the team, and Steve Bruce was in the smiling, back-slapping group. Television cameras zoomed in as captain Cantona tried his best to persuade Steve to go up to collect the Cup in the way that he had been handed the Premiership trophy a week earlier. At Middlesbrough, Bruce was one of the substitutes and so felt part of the side; this time he was not and refused.

So Eric led his colleagues up the famous steps to be handed the trophy by the Duchess of Kent. As he neared the top a Liverpool supporter leaned forward and spat at him twice. It was despicable, disgusting and provocative. Eric turned, paused, raised his hand and wiped away the saliva before

Cantona salutes the Red Army. (Colorsport)

continuing past other rival fans who sportingly cheered him on his way.

The noise inside Wembley was deafening as Eric raised the trophy above his head. A hundred or more skippers had done this before him, but if ever a moment told the world that Eric Cantona was back, it was that act of triumph. Those who doubted that Eric Cantona could cope with the pressures and the provocation had their answer.

United paraded their trophy then passed out of sight of the spectators and into the white-washed tunnel where they ran the gauntlet of television cameras and microphones. Eric had said that he would speak to me after the game and kept his word, but I was not alone. A huge scrum formed around the dressing-room door as Eric, flanked as always by the head of United's security team, appeared.

He blinked at the bright lights, but smiled broadly as he told us what it meant to him to take the Double once again.

Cantona:
I am proud for everybody; everybody from Manchester United: the players, the fans, the staff, Ferguson, Kidd, everybody... my friend Ned Kelly! It was important for us today and to score was also important, but the last goal is always something special. It is historic to win the double Double and next year we will try to win the European Cup, and the Championship, that would be a great double. A treble Double!

He was enjoying his moment as much as we were and replied to the questions from a French interview team for the next minute in his native tongue. When asked to repeat his words in English he replied: 'I cannot remember what I said!'

He expressed his feelings for Steve Bruce.

Cantona:
Steve has been injured for the last few weeks and I feel very sad for him. I wanted him to go up and pick up the Cup but he did not want to. He said 'I have done it before', but I tried to persuade him to go up but he didn't want to. It was a great time for me going to collect it, and it has been a great season.

There is more to come. I play for a club where they have got ambition. I have got ambition and everybody here has ambition so we are never content. We are happy today, but we always look to the future and that is what makes it a great club and I am very proud and happy to be with a club like that. I always want to win like my friends. We know that it is very important for us and everybody in England that we try to win the

European Cup next season. We will try our best and with the young players, and the experienced players we have got, we have a very good chance.

Winning the Cup is different from the Championship. That is a long run so in the end it is normally the best one who wins, in the Cup you have to perform on the day of the game, but we have proved that in the past three years we can handle that situation.

He dismissed the spitting incident.

Cantona:
We all know the difference between Manchester United and Liverpool fans but that is life, it does not matter. It is not important. What is important is the last game and the last victory and we have won today and we are the first team to win the Double twice, so maybe today was more important than when we won the Double two years ago, but it was also important two years ago.

There could not have been a more fitting ending a season in which Eric Cantona had defied all his critics. He had performed to the peak of his ability and behaved impeccably. No longer could the finger be pointed.

Eric came through more traumas in the eight months following his dismissal at Crystal Palace than many of us experience in a lifetime. He had chased the demons away for football, for his family and for Eric Cantona.

Sir Bobby Charlton was one of those who supported Eric during his troubled times and after the final could not hide his delight that so many had been proved wrong.

Charlton:
A lot of people would like to have seen the back of Eric, and we thought that he was not an idiot. He is an intelligent person and if we could salvage things from the situation as it was, then it would be worth it in the long term for us and for the game in this country. We were proved right. He has behaved himself; he has performed wonderfully well and a lot of people have had to eat humble pie over Eric Cantona. He has matured a lot and it is better for Manchester United and for the country that there is someone like this who is playing here, so that we can watch him. I would have hated to have thought of him being somewhere else.

So, Sir Bobby, would I.

Chapter Twelve

....

No *Au Revoir?*

The end of Eric Cantona's love affair with Manchester United was as unexpected as its beginning. If the world of football had been taken by surprise when the Frenchman quit Leeds to sign for Alex Ferguson's side in 1992, it was left in a state of shock four and a half years later when Eric decided it was time to terminate the relationship.

The parting was abrupt, painful and surprising. It stunned Cantona's team-mates who had no hint he would walk out on them when they played what turned out to be their final game together, and it left chairman Martin Edwards and Alex Ferguson close to embarrassment as they broke the news. Cantona had gone, leaving behind thousands of heartbroken and bewildered fans.

The supporters reacted as if he had died, going into mourning, treating his decision to stop playing football like the passing of a friend. They gathered outside the stadium, draped scarves around handrails and fencing, placed replica shirts on the ground, leaving them behind as they walked away weeping. They cried for Cantona.

18 May 1997: Emotional fans outside Old Trafford following the announcement of Cantona's retirement. (Press Association)

The farewell was in some ways typical of Eric, in others unlike him. His love of the spotlight was reserved for the field of play, not for him the grand finale of a fanfare of trumpets, those weeks building up to one last game, then the tearful wave to appreciating thousands from the centre of the field. Others might wish to bow out in that way, not M. Cantona. He was as unpredictable as always, sending everyone the wrong way like those thousands of bewildered opponents he mesmerised with his skill.

His last game in England, or so we are to believe, was played for the benefit of someone less fortunate than himself. The career of David Busst never came within a mile of Eric's achievements and was cut short by an horrific injury. In the unlikely setting of Highfield Road, Coventry, Manchester United's most influential player in decades pulled off his red shirt and handed it to the organisers of the Busst testimonial. Within 48 hours Eric would announce his retirement but he gave not the slightest sign of it that night.

'He was magnificent. The fact that he gave up his time to play in the game was superb. Afterwards I went into the dressing room and Eric was sitting there quietly. I asked him to autograph the shirt and let us use it to raise more money for David, and he did so gladly. Then he spent time meeting members of David's family. There was not the slightest hint that this was his final game for United,' said Murdo Mackay, head of the testimonial committee.

If Busst could have been granted one wish it would have been to be able to continue playing football; Eric was fully fit but was willingly giving up. Had he lost the desire to continue?

News of the retirement reverberated throughout the game.

'It was a bolt from the blue,' was the reaction of Gary Pallister. 'He never let on to the players that he was thinking of retiring, but that is Eric. He keeps his cards close to his chest, but good luck to the guy if that is the way he feels.'

'He never mentioned it to us,' said Nicky Butt, 'that was Eric all over. I didn't know anything about him leaving till I heard the news on the radio as I was driving in Manchester two days later.'

'We heard at the same time as everybody else,' was David Beckham's reaction. 'Eric never said a word. We will miss him because he was such a great player and such an influence on all the young players at the club. I still can't believe he has gone.'

The 1996-97 season began well for Cantona. He continued where he had ended the previous campaign by scoring at Wembley, firing home the first of Manchester United's four goals against Newcastle in the Charity Shield. The Tynesiders had their revenge later in the season, but the hammering United handed out in the pre-season encounter was a clear enough warning of their intentions for the forthcoming Championship. Those who predicted Alex

Cantona opens the scoring for Manchester United in their 4-0 drubbing of Newcastle United in the 1996 Charity Shield. (Syndication International)

Ferguson's side would be beaten to the title by big-spending Newcastle were forced to think again.

The day of the Charity Shield Newcastle paraded their then world record signing Alan Shearer, who cost £15 million, and his striking partner Les Ferdinand, but they could not compete with Cantona and Co. Eric was now fully installed as team captain following the departure of Steve Bruce to Birmingham City. On the field he led by example, off it he was suddenly willing to talk to those of the media he saw regularly, although he was still wary of strangers and kept them at arm's length.

His appearance on BBC Television before the 1996 FA Cup final had blown his cover. His comprehension of English was now obvious and no longer could he hide behind the mask of someone who could not speak the language. Demands for his opinions came from all sides, newspapers, television and radio putting new pressures on the man who had stayed silent for so long. The next nine months would see those pressures increase, Cantona's game suffer and matters reach their unexpected conclusion.

In the days which followed his retirement, newspaper columnists tried to claim there had been signs of what was to happen. It was so easy to be wise after the event, to interpret moments such as the quiet way he reacted after being handed the Premiership trophy, or others when the Cantona body language was supposed to be telling us something was wrong. In fact during the season there had been no real indication it would be Cantona's last at Old Trafford. Far from it.

Six days into the new campaign, which United opened with a 3-0 win over Wimbledon, Eric told me how happy he was with life in Manchester. His radio interview for Piccadilly 1152 a.m. followed days when the sports pages and television screens were filled with reaction to a goal scored by young David Beckham on that opening afternoon. It was an amazing 55-yard shot from inside his own half, hit with power and accuracy over the head of the Wimbledon goalkeeper. It was the kind of goal Eric himself dreamed of scoring:

Cantona:
Yes, I would love to have scored it, everybody would have liked to, but it is very difficult. David is a very good player and he has been picked for the England squad and I think he deserves it for everything he has done since the beginning of last season.

Cantona had seen a change in Beckham, one of his young charges at the club who was being hailed as a future star at both club and international level.

Cantona:
Everybody at the club has seen it. Every game he becomes better, him and the other young players but that is normal. Like us when we were young, the more you play the better you become. Better and better.

Cantona immortalised by Mancunian artist Michael Browne. At his feet are four of the young Manchester United players whose talents he has helped to nurture: (left to right) *Philip Neville, David Beckham, Nicky Butt and Gary Neville.* (Syndication International)

He sounded like the proud father talking about the achievements of his sons. Cantona was willing to heap praise on the young players around him in the United side. It seemed impossible that nine months later he would walk away from Ryan Giggs, Beckham, Gary and Philip Neville, Nicky Butt, Paul Scholes and the other emerging youngsters.

Was this really the happiest time of his life?

Cantona:
Yes, everybody knows it, the happiest time of my career as a footballer. I think it is a wonderful time. So much runs around football here in England and to play for a club like Manchester United and to live in a nice city like Manchester, I like more and more this country, and the people from this country.

He was now captain of Manchester United: did he see this as an added responsibility?

Cantona:
I have always felt that I must have a lot of responsibility even before when I was not captain. I think it is important that everybody feels that they have got a lot of responsibility so that we become stronger as a team, everybody together.

After the sensational start against Wimbledon, United stuttered for three games, drawing with Everton, Blackburn and Derby County before travelling to Leeds to earn their second victory.

Leeds, where the name Eric Cantona made the blood of the home fans boil. They once loved him, but now he truly was the player they loved to hate. In 1992 the Frenchman might have been given the Freedom of the City of Leeds after inspiring the club to their first Championship win in 18 years. He knew as he led his Manchester colleagues out at Elland Road, that afternoon he would once again be greeted like an unwanted guest.

The hostile atmosphere could have contributed to his penalty miss just before half-time. Had he scored, it would have given United a 2-0 lead but we witnessed a rare event – the first penalty Eric Cantona had failed to convert since joining United after 16 previously successful attempts. He would miss one more before his departure, during a win at Ewood Park where, just as at Leeds, he had the last laugh over the goading fans. In both games he managed to score the final goal, 3-2 against Blackburn, 4-0 at Leeds.

The penalty mistakes were later seen as perhaps the first indication that Eric's confidence was eroding. Possibly they were more likely signs of complacency from a player who expected to score every time.

If Cantona was depressed it did not really show. He never lost that walk of stiff-backed arrogance, and still gave the impression that he was staring down that Gallic nose at his opponents as if they were lesser mortals, which was totally opposite to the way he really viewed his fellow professionals.

There were still the times when his brilliance shone through, despite the moments when those who watched wondered what had gone wrong with the maestro. We told ourselves the Cantona of old would have scored instead of putting the ball high over the crossbar, would have found a colleague with a pass rather than losing possession, would have created the opening instead of wasting the opportunity. The Cantona of old? Had the edge really gone from the Frenchman's game?

Those of us lucky enough to see every match he played with United would say it was his consistency rather than the cutting edge of his game which was missing in that final season. He seemed to be battling to produce the performances which had won the hearts of Manchester United followers and football purists throughout the world. Perhaps he tried too hard after convincing himself that he was out of touch. He still created goals with passes of pinpoint accuracy. True, he missed the occasional scoring chance, but this would be forgiven when moments later he produced another piece of Cantona magic to thrill his audience. The problem was they were rarer. We knew he could do better, willed him to do so, and forgave him if he failed.

Despite all this United did well, they were still the best team in the country. Cantona lost his leading scorer's mantle to Ole Gunnar Solskjaer, United's young discovery from Norway, who was full of

Ole Gunnar Solskjaer succeeded Cantona as top scorer in 1996-97. Always full of praise for the Frenchman, here the young Norwegian congratulates him for another successful penalty. (Syndication International)

12 October 1996, Manchester United 1 Liverpool 0: Despite having beaten their biggest rivals, Cantona was disappointed with the match and said of his own performance, 'I forgot that I could play so bad.' (Syndication International)

praise for the Frenchman: 'He is a wonderful player, I cannot believe that I am playing in the same side as him,' he would say modestly. That would seem testimony enough, especially on the day Cantona had inspired a five-man move which ended in Solskjaer scoring his second goal in the home win over Tottenham. The Norwegian glowed in his after-match praise of his teammate.

Perhaps the first real signs that all was not well came on 12 October. United had beaten Liverpool 1-0 at Old Trafford. There was plenty to celebrate. The Saturday morning game had been played in front of the first ever 55,000 all-seater audience at the newly developed stadium. David Beckham scored the winner and United had beaten their biggest rivals.

Eric spoke afterwards. Words which made headlines in the tabloid press:

Cantona:
We did not play very well but we got three points which were very important and everybody will forget the performance and the points will stay all the season. At the end this win could be very important.

The clubs had agreed to an 11.15 a.m. kick-off. Two days later United were to

30 October 1996: Manchester United take on Turkish underdogs Fenerbahce, the team that sensationally ended a 40-year record by beating them 1-0 at Old Trafford in the Champions League. It was their first ever defeat on home soil in a European tie. (Syndication International)

It was a different story, though, when they met FC Porto at Old Trafford in March. United were in devastating form and crushed the much-fancied Portuguese champions 4-0. Here Cantona scores goal number two. (Syndication International)

fly out to Turkey to face Fenerbahce in the Champions League and the early start gave them more time to recover between games. Did this suit the players?

Cantona:
I don't think that is a good excuse. Last year we played a game at twelve o'clock, and two years ago at 11 o'clock, and we played very well and we won. I don't think that is a good excuse for the two teams, for the 22 players, but it wasn't very nice to watch, I think.

What about his own performance. Was he unhappy with his contribution?

Cantona:
Very unhappy, yes. I forgot that I could play so bad. I am very unhappy but we have got a game on Wednesday and next Sunday, and I will try to play better, much better, because I am very, very disappointed about my performance.
    I don't need to be told that I didn't play well, it is true. I realise that myself and I can tell you I am not happy. I am very disappointed.

As it turned out United played brilliantly in Turkey, winning 2-0 with Eric scoring the second goal after a move involving Jordi Cruyff and Solskjaer, two of the players Alex Ferguson had added to his squad the previous summer.
    Disaster followed. On their return to the Premiership four days later they lost 5-0 at Newcastle, Ferguson's heaviest defeat as a manager. Then began a period which tore the heart out of a captain who wanted more success for his side. If Newcastle was bad, a 6-3 upset at Southampton was worse. Then came United's first ever defeat in the home leg of a European tie.
    The record had stood for 40 years and one month, stretching from the pioneering days of Matt Busby to the present. Fifty-five home games without defeat as the mighty clubs of Europe came and saw, and failed. Real Madrid, Barcelona, AC Milan, Ajax had all tried, yet on Wednesday 30 October 1996, Fenerbahce, unfancied Turkish underdogs, got their revenge by stealing a win. United dominated the game for all but one moment, and that was when they conceded a single goal.
    Eric Cantona took the result personally. It was under his captaincy that a proud record had gone. After the game he changed and left the stadium before any of the other players, refusing to speak. The veil of silence once again descended on the man who had told us he was 'very unhappy' 18 days earlier.
    When the European upset was followed by a home Premiership defeat by

Chelsea many thought the chances of retaining the Championship had disappeared along with hopes of qualifying for the later stages of the Champions League. Perhaps those early season predictions that Newcastle would carry away the title would come true.

Alex Ferguson had set out his stall, saying that once the Champions League was behind them United would concentrate on the Premiership. He was right.

The recovery began in December when, four days after a 3-1 home win over Leicester had taken United to fifth place in the table, they went to Austria and in an inspiring performance of attacking football destroyed Rapid Vienna. It was only a 2-0 scoreline but United dominated for long periods with Cantona having a hand in both goals. The first was scored by Ryan Giggs after Eric and Nicky Butt combined to create the opening, the second by Cantona himself following a Beckham pass. The clouds had lifted.

Two goals from Eric in a 5-0 home win over Sunderland saw them start to climb up the table. A penalty from the Frenchman against Leeds took United into second place and by the end of January they were top of the Premiership. They stayed there until the Championship was once again won.

Around this period the doubts about Eric's form vanished. He was as

1 February 1997: Cantona and Gary Neville celebrate the Frenchman's 80th-minute winner against Southampton. Manchester United were top of the Premiership and on course for yet another title. (Syndication International)

influential as always in many games and when the European competition re-started after its winter break he was outstanding. United were drawn against Portuguese champions FC Porto, fancied by many to top the qualifying group ahead even of holders Juventus.

They came to Old Trafford for the first leg of the quarter-final to find United in devastating form. United won 4-0 with Eric involved in all but the first goal which David May scored from a corner. Eric scored the second after he picked up a loose ball 15 yards out. The third came from Ryan Giggs after Cantona, Cole and the scorer himself were involved in a superb move, and Andy Cole sealed the victory with a fine goal after Eric had slipped the ball through the Porto defence.

That 34th-minute strike which gave United their 2-0 lead was the last goal Eric would score in Europe, or so it would seem if he really has walked away from the game.

There was an irony to what would seem to be Eric's final Premiership goal. Since Andy Cole had been brought to the club as his striking partner, Cantona had sacrificed many chances of scoring himself by trying to create goals for the player Alex Ferguson bought from Newcastle. He was aware that all Cole needed to boost a flagging confidence was to score. Some opportunities were taken, others wasted, but when the roles were reversed and Cole cut along the Blackburn by-line to pick out Eric with a pass across goal, he made no mistake and that game was won.

United took a six-point lead into the final stages of the season but in Europe fell to Borussia Dortmund, eventual winners of the competition. Both legs of the semi-final were lost by a single goal and in each game United missed more chances than the Germans. United and Eric Cantona would have to wait another year for European success.

United could wait, Eric would not.

The Premiership title was secured by 6 May, when Newcastle and Liverpool gave up the chase. It was the fourth Championship in the five seasons Eric Cantona had

Cantona lifts the Premiership trophy for an incredible fourth time in five seasons, yet his fixed expression is perhaps a clue that all was not well...
(Syndication International)

been at Old Trafford. The only time they had not taken the title during that period was in 1995, when they lost his services for the latter part of the campaign following the incidents at Selhurst Park.

United fans celebrated in what was becoming a traditional way, gathering in their hundreds outside the stadium, chanting and singing. The party continued throughout five days leading to the closing game of the season, but would turn into a wake by the following weekend.

On Sunday 11 May 1997, Eric Cantona led out his colleagues against West Ham. Old Trafford was packed with a singing, flag-waving mass, and the name of Cantona was chanted and sung more than any other. United won 2-0 on an afternoon when not only the senior side was rewarded for its achievements but so was each of the other teams United field at the various levels of professional football. The first team, reserves, A and B teams each collected a championship cup in a demonstration of total dominance of domestic football. The FA Carling Premiership, the Pontin's Premier League, the Lancashire League Division One and the Lancashire League Division Two. Four teams, four titles.

It was a time to remember, the first occasion in the club's history such a thing had happened. A week later there was another gathering at Old Trafford but this time matters were of a much more serious nature.

On Sunday 18 May, the day after Chelsea had beaten Middlesbrough in the FA Cup final, the media was summoned to an afternoon press conference. The timing was unusual. Such events were reserved for weekdays, so it was not surprising that there was much speculation as cameramen, journalists, photographers and television reporters assembled. Most felt it was to announce a major signing, but why on a Sunday?

Earlier that day United issued a statement to the Press Association for circulation. This was done by mid-morning with conjecture mounting about what would unfold. The timing prompted frantic efforts to round up staff. Many had to be called in from their day off, apologising as they abandoned guests at family gatherings, left friends at the regular afternoon session at their local, or apologetically pulled out of the Sunday four-ball at the golf club. This was obviously no trivial matter.

Speculation had begun to grow once Bryan Robson's Middlesbrough were relegated that Alex Ferguson wanted to add Juninho, the Brazilian midfielder, to his squad. Juninho had thrilled spectators, including the United manager, during a 3-3 draw at Old Trafford a fortnight earlier, and Ferguson had poured out his admiration of the player in his after-match interviews. Was this a hint that he would make a move once the timing was right? Was this the reason they were gathering that afternoon?

Ferguson refused to be drawn into any conversations about Juninho during the period between Middlesbrough's demise and their appearance in the Cup final, saying only: 'There is always speculation surrounding this club and we try not to get involved.' He made it clear that there would be no approaches to Middlesbrough until the Cup final was over. Had he moved so quickly that Juninho was about to be paraded in front of the cameras, before his team-mates even started their empty-handed tour of Middlesbrough on an open-topped bus? Would Juninho be photographed holding aloft a United scarf at the same time that Bryan Robson, the man who had brought him to England, was making optimistic promises that Middlesbrough's stay in the First Division would be brief?

Surely not. If Ferguson considered any approach for the player in the period between relegation and the Cup final as unethical, such obvious haste to sign the player before some 'Boro fans had got home from Wembley was indecent.

There was no Juninho. Whether talk of the Brazilian's possible move to Old Trafford played any part in what was to ensue only Eric Cantona would know. Cantona would certainly have noticed the performance of his opponent as he danced his way through a deluge when 'Boro drew with the champions elect, and his manager's views on the player would not have gone unnoticed. Coming at a time when Cantona was not happy with his own contribution its publicity may not have helped matters.

The critics singled out Cantona for his team's failure in Europe, claiming he had never shown the kind of form he produced in the domestic game when playing on the greater stage. It was true he could have scored a hat-trick during the second leg of the semi-final against Dortmund but he was not alone. The Dortmund defeat sparked speculation that Cantona might move on. A story broke in the *Daily Express* claiming that United were reluctant to look beyond the 12 remaining months of his contract. 'Eric has been invaluable in the last four seasons but you have to consider whether he has seen his best days,' said a club 'source'.

'Extending Eric's contract has been discussed at the highest level and it looks certain nothing will be done this summer. Obviously if Eric starts playing superbly next season it would be stupid not to sit down and sort something out. I don't think the fans will be too surprised, or upset, at the stance.' This was the first hint that Cantona's days at Old Trafford might end.

Even so no one knew exactly what would unfold when Alex Ferguson and Martin Edwards entered the press conference, taking their seats behind a cluster of microphones. Throats were cleared, motorised cameras clicked and whirred, television lights glared as latecomers shuffled into their seats. Silence descended as flashguns fell on the stony expressions of the men in charge of Manchester United.

Edwards:

Good afternoon, ladies and gentlemen. Thank you for attending at such short notice. We have asked you to come along today so that we may announce that Eric Cantona has indicated his wish to retire from football with immediate effect. Eric is away on holiday with his family and is not planning to return to England in the near future. He has, however, supplied us with some comments which will be distributed after this press conference.

Before inviting questions can I just add it is not our intention today to speculate on who may or may not replace Eric.

Eric Cantona has been a marvellous servant to Manchester United. This is a sad day for us and we are here to pay tribute to him, not to talk about his successor or successors.

Would Edwards say when Cantona had told him of his decision?

Edwards:

He came to see me on Thursday but I think you (Alex Ferguson) had an indication before that.

Ferguson:

He saw me on the Wednesday. As the chairman says, it is a sad day for United. He has been a fantastic player to us in the four and a half years he's been with us and we have won six trophies in that period, so it is a sad day.

Was there a chance he might change his mind?

Ferguson:

Well, I don't know how the chairman read it but I thought, whereas in the past, the previous time when I felt he needed a bit of help in that situation, I think he'd made his mind up. He was fairly unequivocal about it. I think I knew deep down that no matter what things I was saying to him he wasn't prepared to take them on board.

What reasons did he give?

Ferguson:

You will find that out in the statement but basically he feels he wants to go out at the top. He feels his four and a half years at the club have been great. He wants to do other things and in that situation it is hard to persuade him.

What about the fans, what will they think?

Ferguson:
They will have great memories of him. They'll be disappointed obviously. It has happened with great players in the past when things have come to an end and we have to get on with life after it.

It will be a big task to replace him but we have a young team and we are quite capable of progressing. It has always been our intention to try to improve the team to meet the requirements needed in Europe, so that won't change.

His influence on the team has been marvellous. He came at the right time. He gave us vision we maybe lacked in terms of winning the Championship. I think we possibly could have done it but he just made the final piece that gave us the vision and composure at important times. He was the scorer of very important goals so it just gelled together after that.

So why had he reached this decision?

Ferguson:
He was disappointed after the Dortmund game, but we were all disappointed. He wasn't the only one, so you wondered how he would get over that. There were a few of us in that boat, myself included, we were all gutted.

When he was at Nîmes, Eric announced his retirement from football but within two or three months he wanted to come back. Would United leave the door open if he was to change his mind?

Edwards:
We keep his registration and if Eric changes his mind we would be happy for him to stay with us.

The fans will want to know if Manchester United have done all they could to persuade him to stay.

Edwards:
When Eric came to see me on Thursday I know I certainly tried to persuade him to stay. I thought he was ending his career prematurely and asked him if he would reconsider, but he seemed to have made up his mind and I think he told Alex similar things.

Do you think you will ever find a player as good as Eric?

Ferguson:
Yes. We have to. This club can't stop still. You talk about great players of eras, decades or seasons. That is what happens in football. Players emerge all the time. This is what we hope at our club, we try to get the best players here.

I would regard Eric as one of the best players at this club without question. Six trophies for a million pounds... put a value on that, please.

I have been very lucky in my signings. I have had some great value but you have to admit and say for £1 million it was incredible.

Legendary players had left Manchester United in the past, but usually with some warning. Because this was premature was it more of a shock?

Edwards:
He is the first player who has not seen his contract out. He has made a decision not to see his contract out so that is a shock in itself. I can only think of Craig Johnston at Liverpool in a similar situation when he was still under contract.

Nothing comes as a surprise with Eric, though, does it?

Ferguson:
Well, something of that magnitude is a surprise, isn't it? He loved his football so that is why it is a surprise.

Had Cantona's form slipped? Was it not true that he had not been as good in the last year as the previous three and a half?

Ferguson:
I wouldn't like to get into that. I don't think that is an issue now. You have to look at his whole career and it has been splendid, he has brought great moments.

Was there one abiding memory for Cantona's last manager?

Ferguson:
There are plenty of memories. He has had some fantastic years for us. It is hard to catalogue them.

Had the chairman thought that Eric would have as big an impact as he did?

Edwards:

Alex thought he would have a big impact, certainly on the footballing side. In a way he started that at Leeds. He was a bit of a cult figure there, they won the league with him coming on as a substitute, but he took over as the main individual. Eric was the name they were all chanting, so I think we had an idea he was a big name, but to some extent it has been a surprise.

The conference ended. Some journalists hurried out of the room to file the sensational story, others gathered in small groups poring over their notes as if in disbelief at what they had witnessed. The cynical smiled; the United fans among the media – and there are some – shook their heads.

Cantona had gone.

As they prepared to write his epitaph he was on holiday at his parents' home in France. He was back where he belonged, where he loved to be, with his wife and their children, playing together in the sun, helping with the chores, getting away from it all.

As for the statement promised at the start of the conference, when this was handed out Cantona's farewell was not obvious to see at first. It was just 90 words sandwiched in the centre of a single page between paragraphs expressing the views of Edwards and Ferguson. It is

Cantona with his son Raphaël. 'I now wish to do other things. I always planned to retire when I was at the top.'
(Syndication International)

doubtful Eric even penned the piece himself, it hardly reads like Cantonic prose:

> I have played professional football for 13 years, which is a long time. I now wish to do other things. I always planned to retire when I was at the top and at Manchester United I have reached the pinnacle of my career. In the last four and a half years I have enjoyed my best football and had a wonderful time. I have had a marvellous relationship with the manager, coach, staff and players and not least the fans. I wish Manchester United even more success in the future.

No *au revoir*, no poetical references to trawlers heading for calmer seas, no mind-bending philosophy to disturb the media for a final time. That, it would seem, was that.

In the days that followed there came speculation that Cantona had quit because the club refused him that contract extension, but there were also claims that he and Ferguson had been involved in a major row. There were opinions that he was upset because he felt he might be pushed out of the spotlight if another big name was signed. It was all gossip.

There were stories that he planned a career in films, and certainly Eric made no secret of his love of the screen. Where Eric Cantona will go from here only he knows, but there is still a feeling that his days in football, and even at Old Trafford, may not be over. That theory was expounded in a harmless comment from one of his team-mates, full-back Denis Irwin. He had last spoken to Eric in the dressing room after the West Ham game. 'He never hinted he was quitting. He never said goodbye… you would have thought he would have said goodbye to us.'

He never said goodbye. Perhaps it is not the end after all?

Cantona – A Statistical Record

Cantona's international career
Debut: 12 August 1987 v West Germany (lost 2-1 in Berlin, Cantona scored)
Total number of caps: 45
Last cap: 18 January 1995 v Holland (won 1-0 in Utrecht)
Total number of goals: 20
Last goal: 26 May 1994 v Australia (won 1-0 in Kobe)
He has never scored a hat-trick for France, but has scored two goals in a match on five occasions.
He has played in 11 World Cup qualifying games (W7, D2, L2), scoring 7 goals, but never played in the finals.
He has played in 11 European Championship qualifying games (W6, D4, L1), scoring 3 goals, and in the finals 3 times (D2, L1).

Cantona in France

Season	Club	Appearances	Goals
1983–4	Auxerre	2	0
1984–5	Auxerre	4	2
1985–6	Auxerre	7	0
	Martigues	0	0
1986–7	Auxerre	36	13
1987–8	Auxerre	32	8
1988–9	Marseille	22	5
	Bordeaux	11	6
1989–90	Montpellier	33	10
1990–1	Marseille	18	8
1991–2	Nîmes	17	2
Totals	Auxerre	81	23
	Martigues	0	0
	Marseille	40	13
	Bordeaux	11	6
	Montpellier	33	10
	Nîmes	17	2
		182	**54**

Cantona in England

Season	Club	League Apps	League Goals	FA Cup Apps	FA Cup Goals	League Cup Apps	League Cup Goals	Europe Apps	Europe Goals
1991–2	Leeds United	6 +9	3	0	0	0	0	0	0
1992–3	Leeds United	12 +1	6	0	0	1	0	5	2
	Manchester U	21 +1	9	1	0	0	0	0	0
1993–4	Manchester U	34	18	5	4	5	1	4	2
1994–5	Manchester U	21	12	1	1	0	0	2	0
1995–6	Manchester U	30	14	7	5	1	0	0	0
1996–7	Manchester U	36	11	3	0	0	0	10	3
Totals	Leeds United	18 +10	9	0	0	1	0	5	2
	Manchester U	142 +1	64	17	10	6	1	16	5
		160 +11	**73**	**17**	**10**	**7**	**1**	**21**	**7**

Cantona's honours

1990 French Cup with Montpellier, beating Matra-Racing 2-1 at the Parc des Princes, Paris

1991 French Championship with Marseille

1992 League Championship with Leeds United
Charity Shield with Leeds United, beating Liverpool 4-3 at Wembley. Cantona scored a hat-trick

1993 Premiership title with Manchester United
Charity Shield with Manchester United, beating Arsenal 5-4 on penalties after a 1-1 draw at Wembley

1994 Premiership title with Manchester United
FA Cup with Manchester United, beating Chelsea 4-0 at Wembley, thus completing the Double. Cantona scored twice
Voted PFA Player of the Year
Charity Shield with Manchester United, beating Blackburn Rovers 2-0 at Wembley. Cantona scored

1996 Premiership title with Manchester United
FA Cup with Manchester United, beating Liverpool 1-0 at Wembley, thus completing the Double – the first side to do this twice. Cantona scored
Voted FWA Footballer of the Year
Charity Shield with Manchester United, beating Newcastle United 4-0 at Wembley. Cantona scored

1997 Premiership title with Manchester United